VALLEY OF THE
GRIZZLIES

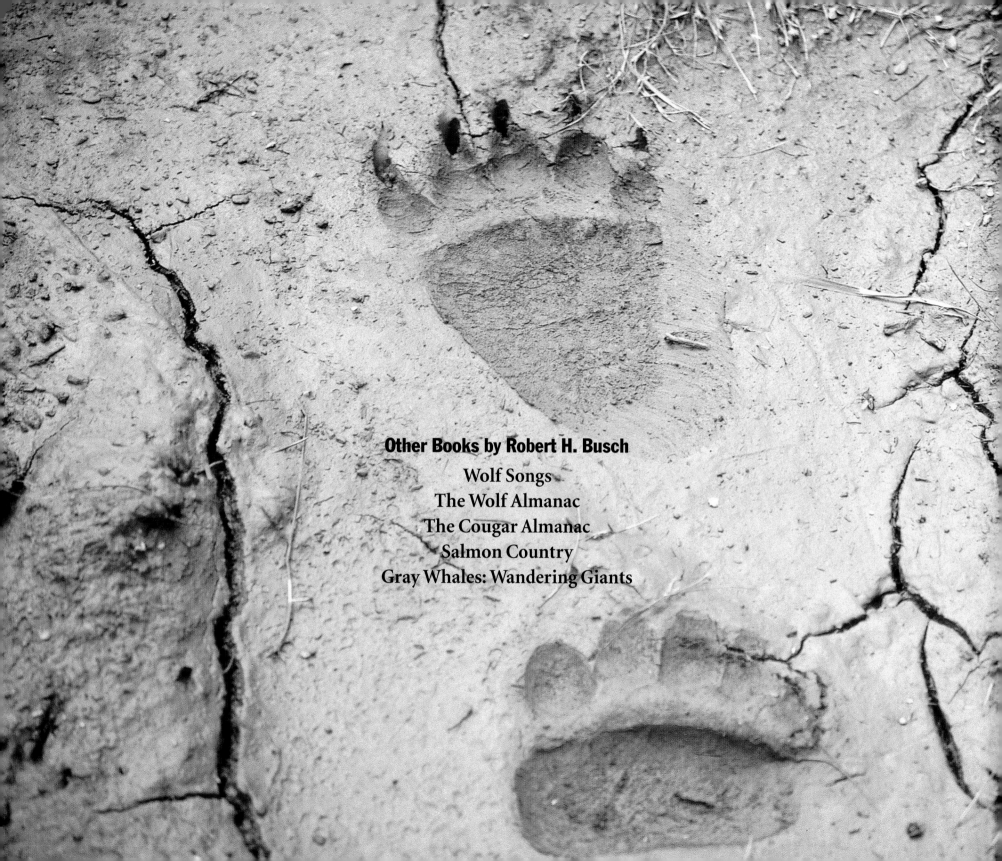

Other Books by Robert H. Busch

Wolf Songs
The Wolf Almanac
The Cougar Almanac
Salmon Country
Gray Whales: Wandering Giants

VALLEY OF THE GRIZZLIES

TEXT AND PHOTOGRAPHS BY ROBERT H. BUSCH

ST. MARTIN'S PRESS

A THOMAS DUNNE BOOK.
An imprint of St. Martin's Press.

VALLEY OF THE GRIZZLIES. Copyright © 1998 by Robert H. Busch.
All rights reserved. Printed in Hong Kong.
No part of this book may be used or reproduced in any manner whatsoever
without written permission except in the case of brief quotations
embodied in critical articles or reviews. For information, address
St. Martin's Press, 175 Fifth Avenue, New York, N.Y. 10010.

ISBN 0-312-19679-2

First published in Canada by Stoddart Publishing Co. Limited

First U.S. Edition

10 9 8 7 6 5 4 3 2 1

For Duke, my best friend

Contents

One

VALLEY OF THE GRIZZLIES

I AM SITTING ON A CLIFF IN BRITISH COLUMBIA AT THE EDGE OF paradise. To my right soars the snow-frosted peak of Mount Ada. Below me, hidden in a cleft of elderly cedars, lie the lonely waters of Lake Mansell. From the lake runs a dark blue ribbon to the sea, the Mansell River. (None of these place names can be found in any atlas: they are pseudonyms, used not to add an air of mystery, but rather to protect the animals of the area from the hunters and poachers who so avidly seek them.)

The Mansell River Valley is choked with wildlife. Packs of wolves pace the black woods at night, their shadows floating through the moonlight. Cougars, wolverine, lynx, and marten all find refuge in the remote wildness of the valley. Golden eagles soar high above, patiently awaiting the glimpse of an easy meal below. And up on the slopes overlooking the valley, one of the last herds of woodland caribou in British Columbia paws the rocky talus for mosses.

The most awesome of all the valley's creatures is the grizzly, one of the largest predators in the world. Attracted by streams red with salmon, dozens of grizzlies congregate here every fall. According to the British Columbia Wildlife Branch, the valley has the densest concentration of grizzlies in all of the interior of British Columbia. It calls the valley "an ecosystem rich in wildlife

(Above) Golden eagles soar over the valley.
(Opposite) The Mansell River, clear and cold, is perfect salmon habitat.

worthy of protection." The local native Indians call it "Valley of the Grizzlies."

It is now August. The air is rich with the earthy odor of dying leaves and rotting vegetation. Walking through the wilderness brings the sobering knowledge that all will be buried under a thick layer of snow within a few short months. It is the time for laying in supplies, for stocking up for the deep freeze of a Canadian winter. It is the time when the grizzly treks down from the high alpine meadows to gorge on the spawning salmon.

At five o'clock in the morning, I jump into a battered four-wheel drive and follow old logging roads for a bumpy two-hour drive. The word "road" is hardly appropriate — you could almost lose a Volkswagen in some of the ruts. Finally I can drive no farther. I hide the vehicle as much as possible, for I want neither hunters nor hikers to follow my trail, and begin a daunting three-hour hike into the Mansell Valley. The brush is sagging with early morning dew, and within a few minutes, I am soaked. But eventually I hear the gurgle of slow-moving water over stones: the Mansell River.

It doesn't look like much in the early morning,

The icy waters of the Mansell River are crystal clear.

when the surface of the river is coated with mist. But as the sun slips over the horizon and the mist begins to thin, a vision of staggering beauty appears. The river itself is crystal clear and the river bottom is cobbled with polished stones the color of raw liver. Huge cedars line the banks, waiting to dive in when they die. The horizon is a halo of wild, untouched mountains.

I have made two camera blinds along one bend of the river, where a gravel bar makes a handy bear-sized fishing platform. One blind is hidden in a thick tangle of riverbank willows and provides a ground-level view of the action. The other is precariously perched on a platform made of two-by-fours about twenty feet up in an ancient pine. Additional two-by-fours along the trunk make a simple ladder up the tree, a perfect platform for bear-watching.

My attraction to the world of nature began at an early age. When I was five or six, my father bought me a pair of ice skates and proudly took me to the community rink to teach me how to skate. I, however, had other ideas, and spent the time on my hands and knees staring wondrously at the bubbles trapped in the ice. (How *did* they stay there?)

When I was older, I was taken on my first fishing trip. My father diverted his eyes for a minute and then quickly discovered that I was nowhere to be seen. Looking around frantically, he caught sight of me perched happily thirty feet up in a pine tree. Climbing trees and looking for birds' nests rated high on my list. Fishing didn't even make it. Poor Dad.

Many years later, when I left my home town of Calgary and relocated to a remote mountain acreage,

Sunset in the
Mansell Valley.

The marshes along
the Mansell River.

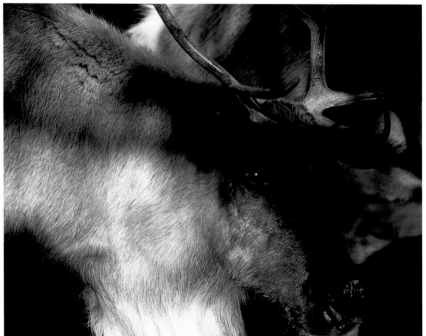

I was often asked why I had moved. It wasn't easy to put my feelings into words then and it's probably harder now. I have learned so much, but miss so little.

So why did I leave the world of ties and takeovers for that of aspens and alpenglow? Part of it has to do with quality of life, that unmeasurable glow that makes it worth getting up in the morning. And part of it has to do with time. In the big city, I was always rushed. I rushed awake in the mornings in order to rush into the big city along with thousands of other two-legged lemmings. I rushed to find a parking spot and then rushed for an elevator. I rushed into my office and then sat nineteen floors of concrete above the real world. It's hard to love concrete. It's also hard to enjoy never having enough time. Perhaps the greatest gift living in the country has given me is the ability to slow down.

I truly appreciate the time I now have to be alone with nature — to savor the rhythms, splashes, and sighs of life on the run. It's like being alone with God.

I also remember the conflicts that I had in the big city with those who did not understand my interest in animals. Some labeled me an animal lover as if it were a negative name, in the same category as child molester or murderer. I once walked around my oil company office trying to collect donations for the local humane society, where I served as president. The entire office, twenty-some wealthy souls, gave a total of five dollars.

It was partly this appalling apathy that led me to retreat to a remote lakeside acreage in the mountain country of central British Columbia. I can do no better than echo the words of biologist Alan Rabinowitz, who wrote in *Jaguar*: "I am running away. Away from the world of people, to a much saner world, the world of animals. I'm doing what I love doing and helping living things that have no control over their own destiny."

My first contact with the Mansell River grizzlies was an indirect one. About three miles from my lakeside home, I had a camera blind set up beside a remote marsh, hoping to photograph bull moose caught in the erotic heat of the fall rutting season.

Early one morning, I equipped my camera with a hefty 300 mm telephoto lens, aimed it at the far edge of the marsh, and waited. And waited. If writing is the loneliest profession, then surely wildlife photography must be number two on the list. To pass the time, I read a few pages of an Agatha Christie mystery between glances through the camera lens. Over the next two hours, I learned a lot about murder, but didn't meet a single moose.

Just as the villain of the story was about to feed his rich aunt a cake garnished with arsenic, there was a crackle from the bushes across the marsh. I quickly dumped the novel and mashed my eye to the camera. The focus was sharp, the exposure was carefully chosen, and I was ready to photograph the majesty of a bull moose in all his glory — when out stepped the biggest grizzly I had ever seen.

A grizzly at close range is an awesome sight, but magnified through a telephoto lens, it's a real heart-stopper. First, I felt my face grow cold as the blood drained away. Then the camera lens began to quiver in my trembling hands. My picture-taking stopped, and I silently cursed myself for my reaction. What was the problem? I had seen bears dozens of times before close-up. Those, however, had been black bears. A huge adult

(Top left) Deer compete to some degree for the same food as grizzlies and occasionally are grizzly food themselves.
(Top right) Woodland caribou live in the higher reaches of the Mansell Valley; note the eartags — this herd of caribou has been intensively studied by biologists.
(Bottom left) A blue heron heads for its roost in the late evening.
(Bottom right) Ducks of all kinds are common in the Mansell Valley.

grizzly is a completely different animal. It was perhaps seventy-five feet away, and its entire bulk said *don't even think of messing with me.*

I assumed from its size that the big bear was a male; I wasn't about to get close enough to find out for sure. It had the shoulders of a linebacker, and I remembered that the distinctive hump on a grizzly's back is a lump of pure muscle. Some people still believe that the hump is filled with water, in some vague association with camels (actually, camels' humps are composed of fat, not water). But I can testify to its being muscle. I once came across a mountain slope that had been bulldozed by a grizzly looking for marmots. Several knee-high boulders had been casually flipped out of place by the muscular bear. When another hiker and I tried to move those same rocks, the two of us couldn't budge any of them.

Through my telephoto lens, I stared at the grizzly's massive paws and was shocked to see that his claws extended out at least two inches. According to most studies, about 85 percent of a grizzly's diet is vegetation. It seems incredible that such a massive beast could be sustained by such a leafy diet; the polar bear is a die-hard carnivore. But if the grizzly lives mainly on grasses

(Opposite) The shoulder hump on a grizzly is pure muscle. (Left) The front claws of a grizzly can reach four inches in length.

and sedges, then why the extra-long claws? I soon found one reason when the bear raked its claws through the bushes, stripping off plump thimbleberries and leaves. It then brought a mittful of munchies to its mouth and delicately picked out the berries with its teeth. The bear looked just like a socialite gracefully nibbling hors d'oeuvres at a fancy party.

After my nerves had settled down a bit, I realized that I still hadn't taken a picture of the bear and quickly snapped a few shots. Big mistake. The bear's excellent hearing had detected the tiny metallic clicks, and his great head swung my way. He spotted me in seconds. I froze and cast my eyes downward, hoping to look as submissive as possible. I tried to speak soft, soothing words to him, but somehow my voice wouldn't work. After a careful scrutiny, he decided I was no threat and resumed feeding.

As I watched, he followed his berry appetizer with an entrée of succulent grasses and bracken ferns. Somewhere in his foraging he must have picked a pawful of wild mint, for the sharp smell of peppermint wafted over the marsh. I remember thinking how ridiculous the big bear looked, grazing along quietly like some overgrown sheep.

By now the sun had leaked over the horizon and dawn began to fill with the cheery sounds of birds announcing the new day. This was apparently his cue to move on. For one horrible moment he stared in my direction one last time. Then he leisurely ambled away, one plod at a time. After a few minutes of rustling bushes, he was gone.

That afternoon I returned to the marsh and left the rotting carcass of a spent salmon as a humble offering to the great bear who had let me enter his wild world for a few minutes. The next morning, the fish was gone. In its place was a gigantic footprint. My size 10 hiking boot fit easily inside it. I stared at the track for a few moments, then packed up my camera gear and began the long hike home.

For three years now I have spent uncounted hours hunched over cameras in the two blinds watching grizzlies feed upon the salmon buffet that miraculously arrives each fall. My observations are collected and compressed in these pages to represent one season in the life of the bears. More than anything else, the past three years have ingrained in me a great respect for the animal that the Blackfoot Indians quite rightly describe as the Real Bear.

(Opposite) The extra-long claws of a grizzly are often used to rake berries from bushes.

Two

THE REAL BEAR

ONE OF THE OLDEST ARGUMENTS IN BEAR BIOLOGY IS WHICH IS largest, the grizzly or the polar bear? Hunting records, as kept by the Boone and Crockett Club, hand the largest bear title to Alaska's Kodiak Island grizzlies. However, these records are not based on weight, but on the summation of skull length and width; compared to polar bears, all grizzlies have very wide faces. Most authorities prefer to use weight as the measurement of choice.

The heaviest bear is definitely the polar bear, the Canadian record of which was a big bruiser weighing 1,780 pounds. The heaviest documented grizzly appears to be one shot on Kodiak Island in 1894, which weighed 1,656 pounds. Grizzlies over 1,000 pounds are very rare; campfire tales of 2,000-plus-pound trophies are pure fantasy. As famed naturalist Adolph Murie wrote in *A Naturalist in Alaska*, "A bear a long distance from a scale always weighs most." The largest Yellowstone National Park grizzly was an 1,100-pound fatso who gained his pear-shaped figure after a steady diet of human garbage at dumps. Most wild grizzlies are in the 300- to 600-pound range, more than enough to put a puny human in his place.

Despite their great weight, grizzlies are surprisingly light on their feet. Because of its larger surface area, a grizzly's foot withstands less than a fifth as many pounds per square inch as a deer's foot. This gives the bear an obvious advantage in chasing prey over snow.

(Above) A good view of the Roman nose of an adult grizzly. (Opposite) The small rounded ears of a grizzly make it look almost cuddly.

It also makes the bear, however bulky, difficult to outrun. Over a short distance, an angry grizzly can easily reach thirty-five miles per hour. One female grizzly in the Cascade Valley north of Banff, Alberta, chased a pickup truck full of park wardens at a maximum speed of just over forty miles per hour for a short distance before she returned to her two cubs.

Male grizzlies are about twice the size of females, and can stretch eight feet from nose to tail and stand four feet high at the shoulders. Male bears are called "boars" and females "sows," a piggy description that I have never found appealing or appropriate.

What is most amazing about the great grizzly is its awesome strength. A big male grizzly may have claws four inches long and canine teeth two inches in length, all of which are used as mighty meathooks. A Yellowstone grizzly was once observed pulling a six-hundred-pound elk carcass through a stream and up a steep bank — a six-hundred-pound dead lift, almost straight up. A few years ago a grizzly visited my remote campsite in the central Yukon. By the time it left, each can in a twenty-four pack of canned pop had been bitten through, a five-hundred-pound box of rock samples had been dragged almost one thousand yards away, and Pierre Berton's book *Klondike*, some two inches thick, had been pierced right through by the bear's teeth.

(Opposite) A grizzly's foot looks amazingly human. (Left) The impressive canines of a snoozing grizzly.

The tracks of grizzlies are composed of huge hindpaw imprints and smaller forepaw prints. The hindprints look amazingly like human footprints. Frederick Dellenbaugh, an artist with the 1871 and 1872 John Wesley Powell expeditions on the Colorado River, wrote in *A Canyon Voyage*: "I . . . was surprised to discover what I took to be the fresh print of the bare foot of a man . . . my companions laughed and warned me to be cautious . . . It was the track of a grizzly bear."

The hindprint of a big male grizzly may be ten to twelve inches long and seven inches wide. If it were a human, it would take a size 20 shoe. The hindprints of a black bear rarely exceed six inches by four inches. One way to distinguish the two bears' prints, aside from size, is the fact that the nonretractable claws leave marks about half an inch in front of the toe pads in black bear prints, while grizzly claws, being much longer, leave impressions one to two inches in front. In addition, a grizzly's toe pad prints almost touch and lie in nearly a straight line. Black bear toe pad prints tend to be more separate and lie along a distinct curve.

A grizzly's front claws are only slightly curved compared to those of a black bear. As a result, grizzlies lack the excellent tree-climbing abilities of their smaller cousins. One of the first to note this was explorer-botanist David Douglas (for whom the Douglas fir is named), who flatly declared in 1824, "This species of bear cannot climb trees."

In fact, when truly ticked off, an angry grizzly might make it up the first ten feet of a good climbing tree. Its sheer bulk usually prevents it from getting much higher, although in 1968 an angry female grizzly protecting her cub in Glacier National Park managed to scramble twenty feet up a tree after a hiker before falling to the ground. Young grizzlies have been documented thirty-two feet high in trees.

Although most grizzlies are a medium brown color, almost every shade from sandy blonde through mahogany has been recorded. Some sport a snazzy two-tone coat with darker paws and ears, like some giant Siamese cat. The typical grizzled appearance is due to silver-tipped guard hairs up to four inches long that shed rain and add insulation to the bear's coat. There do not appear to be any documented records of an albino grizzly.

Grizzlies shed their fur during the spring and summer each year. Naturalist Andy Russell described them in *Grizzly Country*, writing that at this time of molt, grizzlies "take on the look of mountain hoboes — ragged, unkempt, and tattered." The bears often rub their fur off against rough-barked trees like fir and cedar; I sometimes found big Douglas firs in the Mansell Valley with patches of grizzly fur lodged in the bark. Discarded fur is often used by squirrels in den linings. Hidden in the fur at the rear end of the grizzly is a

(Above) The hindprint of a grizzly may be ten to twelve inches long. (Opposite) A single population of grizzlies can show a wide range of coat colors.

(Opposite) A grizzly's sense of smell is about seventy-five times that of humans. (Left) The tiny tail of the grizzly is often barely visible.

stubby four-inch-long tail; it is likely that few people get close enough to the bears to see it.

Of all the great predators, perhaps only the beleaguered wolf is engulfed by more false myths than the grizzly.

Every stuffed grizzly that I have ever seen has been mounted with its lips peeled back in a vicious snarl. However, it is physically impossible for grizzlies to peel back their lips, as they lack the facial musculature necessary for such a movement. When grizzlies do snarl in real life, the mouth is slightly open, exposing the mighty canines.

Another common misconception is that grizzlies have poor eyesight. One reason for the myth is the size of a grizzly's eyes; compared to the huge dish-shaped face, the eyes look like two tiny raisins lost in a vast brown pudding. Actually, although grizzlies are near-sighted, their sight is quite good. When a grizzly rears on its hind legs and appears to peer around as if it were near-blind, it is actually just gaining a lofty viewpoint and a better chance at getting a good scent.

According to University of Calgary biologist Stephen Herrero, "smell is the fundamental and most important sense a bear has." Under the right conditions, a grizzly can detect the stench of a rotting carcass from as far as two miles away. One old blind female in what is now Denali National Park in Alaska was known to have raised at least three generations of cubs with only the directions given to her by her nose and ears. And contrary to popular myth, grizzlies can run downhill. They are also excellent swimmers.

I am often surprised at the number of legends about grizzlies. Perhaps it makes sense that the mightiest of predators should instill a real fear in humans, but the volume of mythology that has evolved from that fear is quite amazing.

Their very size has long given grizzlies an aura of invincibility. Author William H. Wright documented tales of old-time hunters seriously believing that grizzlies "plugged up the bullet holes [in them] with moss to stop the flow of blood." Other bear stories are like fine wine, improving (and sometimes fermenting) with age. These include the numerous tales of wounded grizzlies circling back to attack a hunter from behind. I once asked two bear biologists about these stories and both declared them to be pure myth, on the grounds that grizzlies do not have the mental capacity to seek

revenge. But I'm not so sure we have the means yet to measure animal intelligence or animal emotions, and the sheer number of such tales makes me wonder.

Other stories are easier to dispel. Grizzlies do not hug their victims to death. They do not suck their paws for nourishment when they can't find food or during hibernation. And the meat of the bear's left front paw is not sweeter than that of the right paw. I don't know where some of these stories originated, but I have heard many of them myself, repeated by local hunters and trappers who should know better.

One piece of grizzly lore that I find puzzling is that of tree-scratching. Bear mythology says that these scratches are made by grizzlies declaring their territorial rights for all to see: the higher the scratch, the bigger and more dominant the bear. One nature writer even told of an ingenious young grizzly that rolled a stump up to a tree and stood on it in order to place his scratches higher than every other bear's. Not too likely.

(Opposite) Bear scratches on an aspen tree. (Right) A grizzly's foot withstands less than a fifth as many pounds per square inch as a deer's foot.

I once came across a hillside meadow that seemed to be some kind of bear message center. The meadow faced south and was punctuated with large poplar trees. Within a space just over a hundred feet across, four trees showed bear scratchings. One tree had two patches of scratchings, each about eight inches in diameter, with one about a foot higher than the other. The other three scratched trees each had only a single scratched-out patch, from five to eight feet up on the trunk. All of the scratchings faced in toward the center of the clearing.

What was the reason for so many scratchings in so small an area? If dominance was the reason, wouldn't bears try to place each scratching higher than existing ones on trees? Or did the scratches just state *I am here* to other bears, specifically to other females? The poet in me wondered if it was a romantic rendezvous site. The mountain mystic in me wondered if it was where the great bears came to dance, their huge shadows boogying in the moonlight.

I suspect that most grizzlies scratch trees just to sharpen their claws or as the incidental results of luxurious stretches, just as my cats do on my best sofa. However, some bear biologists have reported that dominant male bears do mark trees more often than subordinates, and that the marking of trees increases during breeding season, so perhaps territoriality and other factors are involved. For a beast as intensively studied as the grizzly, it is surprising how many questions remain.

Some of these questions pertain to bear evolution. The grizzly is a more recent arrival in North America than the black bear. Bears first evolved somewhere in Eurasia, branching off the canine family tree about twenty-five million years ago. About three million years ago, grizzly-like bears evolved. Their descendants strolled over the Bering land bridge to North America only about forty thousand to one hundred thousand years ago.

Biologist D. W. Macdonald believes that polar bears evolved as an offshoot of a grizzly population that was isolated during a period of intense glaciation. A few zoos have reported examples of cross-breedings between polar bears and grizzlies. The offspring resulting from such mismatches are fertile, one proof Macdonald offers that the two giant bears are closely related.

Grizzly taxonomy, in fact, is one of the fuzziest of bear topics. For many years, hunters recognized a difference between the huge Alaskan brown bear and other grizzlies, but physical distinctions were hazy and subspecies boundaries quite arbitrary. The Boone and Crockett Club, for example, drew a line seventy miles from the Alaskan coast and declared that coastal bears within this line were browns and those on the other side were grizzlies.

In the early 1900s, biologists made things even worse and recognized over eighty grizzly subspecies. Today, most accept only two: *Ursus arctos middendorffi*, the big Alaskan brown bear or Kodiak bear, and *U.a. horribilis*, a catch-all that includes all the other grizzlies in North America. Names such as the Shiras bear, Toklat grizzly, and Kluane grizzly are local labels with no scientific merit.

Grizzlies are not truly territorial, but they do roam indistinctly defined areas in search of food. Territories

(Opposite) The impressive bulk of a male grizzly.

may range from five to fifteen hundred square miles in area, depending on the availability of food. Male grizzlies tend to roam over larger territories than females. Some of the smallest bear territories on record are on the various Alaskan islands, where rich diets of salmon and berries allow dense concentrations of grizzlies. In the Kodiak National Wildlife Refuge, on Alaska's Kodiak Island, there is a cozy density of one bear per one and a half square miles.

When relocated, grizzlies usually try to return to their home territory. But not always. An Alberta grizzly was relocated in October 1994 from its territory near Hinton to a new spot some six hundred miles to the north. Almost a year later, the wayward bear was shot by a hunter near Dease Lake in northwest British Columbia, over nine hundred miles away. "For whatever reason, his internal navigation system went haywire and he probably thought he was heading home," says Tony Hamilton, a B.C. bear biologist.

Through most of the year, grizzlies are loners, padding slowly through their territories in search of food. But in late spring to early summer, males feel the urge for female company. In central British Columbia, most grizzly matings take place in June, but across the rest of the continent, matings may occur from May through July.

Each male grizzly may breed with more than one female, and the bears stay physically coupled for up to forty-five minutes. Occasionally the female seems to lose interest halfway through the mating process and begins to amble off or even to begin grazing, with her mate still hanging on for dear life. The males rarely stay with their mates for more than a few days and play no active role in raising the young.

The grizzly's gestation period is about 235 days. A mother grizzly displays delayed implantation, whereby a new embryo floats freely for months before finally attaching itself to the uterine wall to grow and develop. The delay allows female grizzlies to fatten up by themselves in the fall without having to tend to pesky cubs. Once the cubs are born, the female's body is well equipped to handle their heavy nutritional demands. Females in poor condition may not conceive at all.

Female grizzlies are not sexually mature until four to eight years of age, males until five to ten years. Females sometimes breed every other year, but often only every three or four years. (The average interval between litters in British Columbia is three years.) The grizzly is the slowest-reproducing of all the great predators in North America. According to the World Wildlife Fund (Canada), "the removal of even a single grizzly can have a serious biological impact on a particular bear population." Unfortunately, far too many government wildlife branches were late in recognizing this important factor in grizzly management.

Grizzly cubs are born in late winter through early spring; in central British Columbia they usually arrive in late January. A grizzly's first litter is often just a single cub, but later litters may range from one to four, averaging two. At birth, the tiny cubs weigh only about a pound, but they grow quickly on milk ten times richer than cow's milk. The cubs' eyes open at about twenty-one days, and the little bears are fully weaned by about twenty-four weeks. When the bears emerge from the den in spring, the cubs are already hefty little fellows eager to play and to eat.

The grizzly's digestive system is dreadfully inefficient, and its life is thus one long search for food. The list of grizzly food items is a lengthy one, including grass, sedges, bulbs, berries, bark, rodents, birds, insects, and fish. As naturalist John Muir wrote in *Our National Parks*, "To him almost everything is food except granite."

In early spring, grizzlies scrounge winter-killed deer, moose, and caribou with great success. In late fall, the big bears are not above raiding squirrel caches for nuts and seeds. In Yellowstone National Park, squirrel caches of whitebark pine cones provide a significant proportion of the grizzlies' diet. Pine cones don't sound very substantial, but some of these caches reach amazing sizes; biologists found one that contained almost three thousand cones.

Almost all bears love carrion, but individual bears sometimes develop highly individual food preferences. One Yellowstone grizzly preferred to kill live elk, disdaining the numerous elk carcasses available to it. Another grizzly's kill was once witnessed by a Yellowstone park ranger. The bear had surprised a herd of elk crossing the Madison River and killed one of the cows with a single mighty blow to its head with a front paw. The adult elk was killed instantly, the ranger said, in "an explosion of brains, blood, and bone fragments." Young fawns and calves, however, are more common grizzly fare.

Berries of all types line the trails in the Mansell Valley.

FÜTTERE
NICHT, DU
TÖTEST DEN BÄR!

A FED BEAR
IS A DEAD
BEAR

**A B.C. Parks sign against
the feeding of bears.**

Naturalist Andy Russell discovered that southern Alberta grizzlies dine on one of the more unusual of grizzly food items — ladybugs. Grizzlies in Alaska have been observed digging out clams. Other grizzlies have been found feasting on explosions of army cutworm moths, tiny food for such a huge beast. "They will eat some of the lowliest crud in the world, but they still know a square meal when it comes along," Thomas McNamee wrote in *The Grizzly Bear.*

Unfortunately, many grizzlies also learn to love garbage. In Alberta's Banff National Park, grizzlies regularly used to travel twenty-five miles to feed upon garbage before the dumps were made bear-proof.

Across most of British Columbia, local dumps in rural areas are neither fenced nor equipped with bear-proof containers, forging a disaster waiting to happen. Most garbage-eating bears end up shot by panicky humans who don't want bears hanging around. As the B.C. parks department says, "a fed bear is a dead bear."

The fall is a desperate time for grizzlies, as they must eat prodigious amounts of food totaling up to forty thousand calories per day in preparation for winter hibernation. By late fall, a grizzly's weight may be 85 percent higher than that in the spring. By the end of hibernation, half of the bear's weight may have been devoured by the bear's metabolic needs. Bears that do not gain sufficient weight during the fall often die during winter.

During the fall, the fur on grizzlies' backs grows thick for extra insulation. Their heartbeat begins to slow from the normal ninety-eight beats per minute to ten. During hibernation, it may slow even further to a sedate eight beats per minute.

In British Columbia, late October is the time when most grizzlies start seeking out a den in which to hibernate over the cruel Canadian winter. (Technically, grizzlies are not true hibernators, often awakening from their deep sleep to move about or even to emerge from the den. Winter loggers and snowmobilers are increasingly causing problems by disturbing sleeping grizzlies. An awakened grizzly may not return to its den and unless it can dig another one, it may die. One grizzly disturbed from its den near Rogers Peak in British Columbia didn't bother to dig a new den at all. A park ranger found it curled up under a mound of snow right on an abandoned spur of the Canadian Pacific Railway. The bear lay there undisturbed until April, when it ambled away from the unusual den site.)

Most dens are situated to ensure early snow cover and tend to be at high elevations, ranging from three thousand to ten thousand feet. They are often dug under large rocks or tree roots, with the entrance just large enough to admit the bear. A typical den was discovered by Andy Russell near the head of Cataract Creek in the Rockies of southern Alberta and he described it in *Grizzly Country*: "The entrance tunnel sloped down for perhaps eight feet at about a twenty-five degree angle, and then it turned laterally along a sunken rock ledge for another six feet before opening up into a chamber approximately eight feet wide and three and a half feet high."

One ambitious Alaskan bear once dug a den a total of nineteen feet long with a comfy six-foot by nine-foot chamber at the end. The denning chamber is often elevated, providing both a heat trap and good drainage if the den's roof should leak. Dens may be lined with grass or soft tree boughs, sometimes to a depth of about ten inches. Although some grizzlies reuse old dens, more often they dig new ones each year.

When grizzly cubs emerge from the den in the spring, they have a hard life ahead of them. Cub mortality is very high. At the McNeil River State Game Sanctuary in Alaska, a study between 1971 and 1974 found that 40 percent of the cubs did not survive to the age of two. Some cubs died by drowning in swift rivers; some lost their footing and fell off steep cliffs; and others fell prey to disease, injury, or predation by bigger bears.

Later on in life, other perils arise. In a 1975 to 1982 study of ninety-five grizzlies in Yellowstone National Park, one in three of the bears died during the period. Eighty-four percent of the deaths were caused by humans.

Although there is one record of a zoo grizzly living to the age of forty-seven, most wild bears are lucky to reach twenty-five. Bears are aged by counting the growth rings in their teeth. This was known as early as 1860 by John "Grizzly" Adams, who wrote: "every year a ring is added to its tusks," an amazing observation for an unschooled outdoorsman. The oldest wild grizzly on record in British Columbia was thirty-four, a ripe old age for a Real Bear.

Three
BEAR-WATCHING

(Above) A serene stretch of the Mansell River in autumn garb. (Opposite) A subadult, soaking wet after a fall rain.

BY LATE AUGUST, BRITISH COLUMBIA IS AN EXPLOSION OF color. It's as if some wild-eyed painter took all the pastels in his palette and threw them to the winds. From my perch up in the pine beside the Mansell River, I often passed the time by trying to name the various shades that surrounded me: cinnamon, vermilion, apricot, peach, burnt orange. My personal favorite (for various reasons) was tequila-gold. The firs and pines were a swirl of greens and blacks, filled with shadows and shadows within shadows. On most days, the sky overhead was a ceiling of the purest Wedgwood blue. On the forest floor were bursts of color whose very names were a joy to the ear: forget-me-not, fireweed, wild rose, crocus, bunchberry, and Indian paintbrush.

My first two days of bear-watching on the Mansell River were filled with lots of frustrations, but no bears. Maybe it was too early; the peak salmon run had only begun farther downstream. Or maybe the bears knew I was there. After hours of my stumbling through waist-high brush, I'm sure every animal within two miles heard that it had a human visitor. I'm also sure that they could smell me — soaked to the skin with morning dew and sweat, I probably smelled even worse than the rotting salmon.

Although I had no luck with grizzlies for the first few days, I was amazed at the other wildlife that emerged from the forest. I learned long ago that the best way to watch animals is not to chase them, but to sit still and let them go about their ways. A startling flash of metallic blue would announce the arrival of a Steller's jay, which would critically examine me with its head cocked to one side, and, after deciding I was neither edible nor dangerous, would hop onto the forest floor to search for seeds. Or a whirr of high-pitched chatter would shatter the silent wilds when a squirrel angrily informed me that it was *his* tree I was sitting in.

The long hikes into the valley taught me to really see what was around me. It was like entering Alice's looking-glass into a new world. One day beside the trail I spotted a giant spiderweb bejeweled with drops of dew. I couldn't believe that I had never seen it before. Another time I was busy rushing to get to the blinds when I felt a sharp stab of pain in one finger. I had stumbled over a wasp's nest, hidden under a tree root, and had been warned by its irate tenants. How many times had I walked that trail before and never noticed the nest? It took a few weeks to learn to ease my pace, and when I did, my aimless eyes began to see.

(Above) A spider web glistens with morning dew. (Opposite) By late August, the creeks are filled with salmon.

Behind a large boulder, I found a whole spectrum of greens in a ferny hollow filled with mosses and fiddleheads. The rock itself was laced with veins of shining white quartz, comprising a mosaic of color that only nature could have painted.

One afternoon I watched a group of grouse materialize from the grasses. The male sported an erect black neck ruff, and his tail was spread wide in display. The drab females, three in all, didn't seem too impressed, or perhaps they were being coy, and pecked away at the dirt. When the birds spotted me, the females quickly flew off into the nearest tree. The male, however, started pecking once at the dirt and then trotting off three steps, and then pecking again. He did this for a stretch of about twenty feet, until I realized that he had successfully lured me away from the womenfolk.

Another day I spotted a great horned owl perched in a big cedar that stood guard over the river. It wasn't the sight of the big bird that attracted me, though. It was the sound the bird was making, a squeaky *mweep mweep* that I have never heard before. I told a bird-freak friend in Calgary about the call, and he haughtily informed me that great horned owls do not make that kind of sound. But I heard it.

It wasn't until the third day at the gravel bar that I finally saw my first Mansell grizzly feeding. I never heard him come and was startled when I saw a huge brown bear suddenly appear from the meadow's edge above the bar. He stood stock-still for almost three minutes and looked around carefully before descending to the openness of the bar. Ninety percent of the time, grizzlies prefer to stay in the cover of forest and only venture out in the open in search of food.

That day two other bears also arrived at the bar. What had attracted them? I suspect that the numbers of dead salmon on the bar had finally reached the point where their smell was able to be detected from afar. Or perhaps the bears were just reacting to some internal clock that told them now was the time to go down to the river.

The three bears took up separate and distinct feeding territories on the bar, and always kept an eye out for intruders approaching their turf. They only stayed for a few hours, perhaps because they had detected my smell and were apprehensive at the strange odor. But those few hours were some of the happiest I have ever spent, for they were the start of a long and rewarding relationship that still exists today.

Flushed with the success of my initial encounter, I returned again and again to the gravel bar, as did the bears. After a couple of weeks of observation, I learned to distinguish perhaps half of the eight or nine bears that came to feed there. Most were a deep chocolate color, but one young female had a distinctly light coat. I, of course, dubbed her Blondie. Another female was the unfortunate mother of two horrible twin cubs, which I called the Terror Twins. These two little goofs were always in trouble, and their poor mother seemed to almost wring her paws in anguish.

One day I watched as the Terror Twins decided to say hi to their neighbors, and strolled playfully over near a big male. Their mother was there in a flash,

(Opposite) Choosing a fishy meal. (Left) A blue heron, common wherever there are fish to be found.

woofing a sharp danger signal that sent them scurrying back into the woods. Luckily, the bear was busy stuffing his face with salmon, and only gave the cubs a quick warning glance. A few steps closer, and the cubs probably would have been added to the menu. Despite a scene in the popular movie *The Bear*, in which a male grizzly adopted an orphaned cub, big males are well known as cub killers.

(Opposite) Attila, the biggest bear on the bar.

Most of the bears were around 350 pounds, a respectable weight for grizzlies, but hardly record-setters. It's hard to imagine a Kodiak grizzly, the Schwarzenegger of the grizzly world. Pumped up on fat salmon and rich berries, these bears sometimes pass the 1,100-pound mark. The Mansell grizzlies had much the same diet, so why didn't they reach the same size? (It's always frustrating watching wildlife — I find that I often emerge after a season in the bush with more questions than answers.)

The biggest of all the bears was Attila, a huge male that weighed probably close to 550 pounds. A bear twice his size is almost unimaginable. Another bear that I was able to name was not distinctive because of his looks, but due to his temper. I called him Grumpy. This guy had a permanent bad attitude. Whenever another bear even took a few steps in his direction, he would growl and charge. I often wondered if he was sick.

The first bears that I saw at the bar were scroungers, dining on the numerous dead salmon littering the gravel bar. Most used the same feeding technique: standing right on top of a dead fish with their front paws and ripping out flesh with their teeth. Later, I saw that some of the bears had become quite the gourmets.

One liked to suck out the eggs from live spawning salmon, leaving the rest. Another ate only one chunk out of the fish's flanks. I never saw a bear discard a fish entirely, even though the rotting smell to me seemed disgusting. I couldn't imagine taking a bite out of something that smelled like that.

Many of the bears had distinctive fishing techniques, and Blondie seemed to be the most successful. Her specialty was standing on a gray-black island of rock that protruded about a foot above the water surface. When she spotted a salmon swimming close enough to the rock, she launched herself into a mighty leap and pinned the unfortunate fish under her two front paws.

Grumpy, of course, had to be different. He would stand in the shallows, in only about six inches of water, and wait for a fish to drift by. Then he would jab at it with his head and grasp the fish directly with his mighty jaws. These floaters were the most battered of all the fish, rotten completely through, and covered with white slimy fungus. Maybe this is why he was grumpy.

Attila always took the best spot, a small pool that lay beneath a foot-high set of rapids. Here, the salmon would gather and rest a bit before trekking on upstream. Talk about fish in a barrel. Attila merely stood there and chose his fish, pinning it with one fry-pan sized paw and chomping it down with obvious relish.

All of the bears seemed to be right-handed, using only their right paws to move fish around in order to get a better hold or to turn over rocks to get at rotten salmon morsels tucked underneath. Interestingly, both Alaska's Inupiaq Inuit and Greenland's Thule Inuit report that the polar bear is left-handed.

Despite some naturalists' observations to the contrary, I never saw a bear swat a fish right out of the water. And despite the fears of some commercial fishermen, the number of live salmon caught by the bears was insignificant compared to the human haul downstream. A good catch for one day of fishing by a bear was usually about four live salmon; Attila sometimes caught a few more due to his choice spot. Compared to the millions of salmon caught by humans, the total caught by grizzlies and black bears is of little consequence.

Late summer is usually a safe time to hike in central British Columbia as far as bugs go. In June, it is impossible to sit outside for hours on end without getting eaten alive, but by August most of the bugs are gone. One day at the gravel bar a great humming herd of mosquitoes discovered me while I was watching the bears and made my life more than miserable. Mosquito repellent was not among my August gear, and the little monsters had quite a feast. I tried closing my eyes to them, but that made it rather difficult to read. And without reading, there was no way I could sit in a camera blind for six hours at a stretch. Every time I closed my book, I squashed a few of the critters between the pages. The local library probably wondered what I had done to their books.

Finally, I could stand it no longer and swept my arm around my head to scare the bugs away. I did it without thinking about how the bears would react to a human arm suddenly appearing above the willows and waving about wildly. Two of the closest bears spit out their breaths in an explosive huff and then stood on their hind legs for a better look at this weird bush that had sprouted arms. One took a few steps in my direction and then stood up again. I froze, and after a few minutes they resumed fishing. That was the last time I waved away bugs.

I soon learned that even though I had been so careful, the bears knew that I was there. One morning Attila appeared out of the brush and stood looking out over the gravel bar, scanning the area for potential danger. You could almost see him searching his memory banks for familiar landmarks: *Oh yes, there's the fallen cedar, the big rock, the idiot with the camera, the gravel bar . . .* He looked straight at me a few times, and though I was hidden by a thick tangle of brush, he knew I was there all right.

Just to test my theory, early one morning I moved the second camera blind from down in the willows to a spot a few hundred yards away. When Attila arrived an hour or so later, he did his scan and then stopped quickly, did a double take at the unfamiliar blind location, and then crashed back into the undergrowth.

(Above) The elusive cougar — largest predator in the Mansell Valley after the mighty grizzly. (Opposite) Chasing salmon in the shallows.

Some of my happiest hours came watching the Terror Twins. Like all kids, their energy was boundless, and they romped over the gravel bar like human children let loose in a playground. Everything was grist to their mill. A limp fish skeleton became a great toy when gripped in the cubs' teeth and swung around like a smelly Frisbee. Tugs-of-war with tree branches were common games, and "you're it" drove their poor mother totally nuts. I often noticed that the two mock-attacked each other with mouths wide open, the sign of bears at play.

Biologists will tell you that play serves to strengthen social bonds and teaches survival skills that youngsters will later need as adults. Sometimes. These two little twerps were just plain having fun. Dashing over the bar, the two cubs would chase each other with little respect for the bigger bears, which often look on unprotected cubs as prey. One glance from a larger bear toward the cubs was enough to bring their mother on a run, woofing them out of danger.

Trumpeter swans at sunset.

Although grizzlies are usually territorial to some degree, the rule seems to break down at intensive feeding areas like garbage dumps and fishing holes. However, the social hierarchy prevails, and the prime spots on the gravel bar were always taken by the big male grizzlies. Adult females seemed to come next on the list, and then subadults. The Terror Twins came last.

The communication among the bears was subtle, but noticeable. Most of the time, a mere glance from a superior bear was enough to make a subordinate back off. There was also a distinct bear body language that I learned to read. Dominant bears often postured, walking very erect, with head held high. A direct stare from one of these guys usually sent other bears back into the bushes. Bears low on the totem pole held their heads low and always seemed to be checking over their shoulders to see if higher-ups were around. Vocalizations were rare, and were usually confined to low growls used to underline a bear's anger. When you weigh 350 pounds, you don't have to say too much.

Late August is the time when other species besides salmon arrive in the Mansell Valley. One day a metallic honking alerted me to the sight of five trumpeter swans gracefully floating overhead. Many of the local lakes are important fall feeding sites for the big birds. It is shocking to think that a few decades ago, only a few dozen trumpeters were found in the entire province.

The comeback of the trumpeter swan is one of the few success stories in wildlife conservation that Canada has. The white pelican and nine other species have been downlisted on the endangered species list, and the tiny swift fox is now back home on the range on the Canadian prairies, but for over 250 other species, the future doesn't look quite so bright.

The arrogance of humans and their blindness toward the plight of other species always surprise me. The sight of huge white swans gliding aloft warmed my very soul that day. I can't imagine a world without swans, or whales, or grizzlies. It would be a world impoverished and lacking in color, a vast, empty room.

The Terror Twins, in a minor disagreement over ownership of a tree branch . . .

. . . and the victor hauls away his prize.

The moose is the largest animal in the Mansell Valley.

One of the other species that I spent a lot of time watching was the moose, monarch of the marshes. I never did see any bull moose in my first year on the Mansell River, for they tended to be wary and kept to remote thickets. But I did see a number of cows and calves. Even a dedicated animal-lover would have to admit that the moose is one of the ugliest beasts in the forest. Knobby knees, a ridiculous little excuse of a tail, a big snout like an overgrown pig — moose always look like they're composed of nature's spare parts.

I once came across a young moose that was obviously sick. It was thin, and its coat was dull and stringy. Worst of all, it was softly moaning in a dry, buzzing voice that I have never heard used by any other moose. I went home to get my gun and end the poor animal's misery, but when I returned, it was gone. I can only hope that it died a quick death.

And strange as it might sound, I hope some predator ended that moose's life. For that is the place of grizzlies and wolves and cougars — to weed out the sick, the diseased, and the dying. A quick death from predation is certainly preferable to weeks of suffering from disease. After a bit of research, I suspected that the moose had been infected with a brain, or meningeal, worm, a tiny thing whose Latin name is longer than the worm itself: *Parelaphostrongylus tenuis.*

Originally, in North America moose haunted the northern forests and white-tailed deer the southern woods. High southern populations of humans and the clearing of northern forests combined to push the deer northward and the moose south. In central British Columbia, moose were rarely found south of the city of Prince George until the turn of the century. The local Indian peoples have no word for moose in their native vocabulary. Moose reached the Mansell area in about 1912, and today their range stretches to the United States border, five hundred miles south of their original limit.

Unfortunately for moose, white-tailed deer sometimes play host to the tiny brain worm. The worm passes through deer feces onto vegetation, where it is gobbled up by foraging moose, then makes its way into the moose's spinal tract and into its brain. Strangely enough, deer seldom die from brain worms, but moose often do.

In mid-September, a new bear appeared at the gravel bar, which I now thought of as the Salmon Bar. She was an old adult female, with three big cubs. Maybe it was because she had a large family to defend, but the new bear seemed overly fearful and cautious around the established members of the Salmon Bar. It was obviously not her territory, and she treaded very carefully around the "owners" of the bar. One horrible afternoon, I found out why.

The new bear had hung around the fringes of the feeding territory, where perhaps too little food could be scrounged for her three cubs. For whatever reason, she gradually edged closer and closer to Attila's favorite fishing pool until she took one step too close to the big male. One minute she was safe and the next she was charged by over five hundred pounds of furious bear. The two grizzlies roared and reared, with the big male's teeth only an inch away from the female's jaws. Her three cubs skidaddled away from the ruckus and hid behind a fallen cedar, bawling out their fear. Attila was mad, and suddenly gripped the female's jaws in his own. I heard a gurgling sound and drops of blood appeared at the corner of the female's mouth. She was obviously hurt, but gamely battled on for a few minutes, charging the big male repeatedly until she finally gave up. Even I could read the signals when her head suddenly lowered and she looked off to one side. Attila stood still and stared at the beaten female as she slowly backed up and then walked up the river a ways. Her cubs quickly scrambled after her. I never saw any of them again.

A family of Canada geese, surprised in the early morning.

I sometimes wondered if it would be better to move my blinds, depending on the wind direction, so that the bears would not be bothered by my smell (if indeed they were). I tried wetting a finger and holding it up in the breeze, but couldn't figure out which way the wind was blowing. Maybe the finger was too dirty. I remembered reading about natives using a bag of firepit ashes to test the wind, and so one day I shook a bag of ashes into the wind. I found out which

way the breeze was blowing all right — right into my face. That night I burned my Boy Scout outdoors badge.

Whenever I hiked into the Mansell Valley, I was careful to wear the same clothes. Once I knew the bears were aware of my presence, I tried to vary my routine as little as possible. A thick woolen shirt was always covered with a thin brown windbreaker. My pants were always a favorite khaki pair, and my boots were the same old beat-up ones that I have used for years. It may not have made any difference to the bears, but it was important to me that I disturb them as little as possible.

I used two cameras, a Minolta equipped with a 70-210 mm zoom lens, and a Nikon with a fixed 300 mm telephoto lens. All of the photography was done during the daytime, although I tinkered with the idea of using a spotlight or flash for evening shots. But that would have definitely disturbed the bears, and so I never tried it.

Usually I quit the bar after a day of bear-watching, and started the long trek home at around six o'clock. One night, however, I did try camping out in one of the camera blinds. It was in mid-September, and the day had been unusually warm. My sleeping bag at first seemed superfluous, but the chilly night later made me glad that I had brought it. I obviously couldn't sleep in my cramped tree blind, so I scooped out a shallow bed in the lower blind that was hidden in willows near the river. As I lay there, I realized that I was, in fact, sleeping as a bear would sleep, hidden in a thick tangle of brush in a temporary bunk.

Bears, of course, do not stop feeding when night falls, and the evening was an exciting one, punctuated at intervals with the rude sucking noises of bears marching across the mudflats beside the gravel bar. A barred owl hooted its four-tone call in the distance, and a bat entertained me with its ability to hit the brakes in mid-flight and angle off to catch some tiny fly.

The air smelled of pines, with the sulfurous smell of swamp gas drifting in from time to time from the marshes downstream. Above me, it was black, blacker than city folks can ever imagine. And on the horizon, wavy bands of lime green made up the aurora borealis, the northern lights that add a surreal Dali-like dash to

(Opposite) Digging for roots.
(Left) Soaking wet, a grizzly plods through the thick forest along the Mansell River.

**(Opposite) A barred owl.
(Right) A young buck mule
deer stares at my intrusion.**

the sky. Despite the proximity of a dozen hungry grizzlies, I have never slept better.

After I got to "know" the bears a bit, I realized that an unusually high number were subadults. There were relatively few adult females and very few huge males. This is usually the sign of an overhunted or overpoached bear population. Even here, almost as remote a valley as there is in British Columbia, the hand of humans had reached its choking grip. And so I worried — especially about the future of the Terror Twins.

A distressing number of the local loggers and truckers were famous for shooting bears on sight, black or grizzly. In my first year of living in central British

Columbia, I knew of three grizzlies shot out of season by loggers. Highly illegal, but with no conservation officer for a hundred miles, who's to stop them? In the remotest parts of central and northern British Columbia, it's the redneck hunter who rules when it comes to wildlife.

Signs would be of no help, for many of the rod-and-gun types choose not to read them. Some of them probably *can't* read them. I'll never forget an irate neighbor's comment after a fly-in hunter ignored a bright red NO HUNTING sign and shot a deer right on my neighbor's private access road: "I know it's wrong to generalize — I know that some of these guys might have been to M.I.T. — but I bet a lot of them can't even spell it."

Grizzly scat.

Sometimes on the hike home from the Salmon Bar, I sampled some of the berries on which my bear buddies gorged themselves. Thimbleberries, plump but tart. Wild raspberries, incredibly sweet with tiny crunchy seeds that stick in your teeth. And huckleberries, so ripe they always look like they're about to burst. Covered with light cream, with just a dash of Cointreau, a wild berry buffet is utterly delicious.

Occasionally when looking for berries I would find bear scat. I never learned to tell black bear scat from that of grizzlies (I assume that grizzlies leave a bigger pile), but I could sure tell what they had been eating. A grass and leaf diet resulted in firm cylindrical feces. A diet rich in berries resulted in a dark mushy pile that looked like a runny cow pie. My hiking boots can confirm that the latter predominated along the trail.

Late September brought hard cold rains. The bruised blue sky often became too dark for photography, and I sat cursing the ugly weather. Despite the fact that the bears were often soaking wet to begin with from standing in the frigid river, they seemed agitated by the continual downpour. It was on such a damp and dismal day that I almost made a fatal mistake.

To put it delicately, after hours of bear-watching, I felt the urge to go "water a tree." (The sound of the drizzling rain probably didn't help any.) I didn't want to do this under the tree my camera blind was in, so I hiked off a bit in the bush. I thought I heard a strange sound, but dismissed it as the rain in the trees. Wrong. A second later, a definite angry, guttural cough reached my ears. I froze and tried to place the sound, and then I knew. There, not thirty yards away, stood Attila, the biggest bear on the bar. I was in big trouble.

I had inadvertently wandered too close to the trail leading to Attila's private fishing hole, and he made my trespassing crystal clear. His great head swung from side to side and I tried desperately to recall what that meant in bear lingo. Bluff? Attack? I couldn't remember. Then he charged, covering ten feet in a couple of bounds, parked his huge front feet, walked off to one side, and then charged again.

I took a deep breath and willed my heart to start again. He hadn't touched me, so he probably just wanted me out of there. I stared straight at the ground and then slowly backed up a couple of steps. Attila watched me and then casually walked back down to the bar. Retreat with dignity, on both sides. I had been lucky.

Four

GRIZZLY ATTACKS

ONE OF THE MOST INTERESTING ASPECTS OF THE GRIZZLY'S nature is its restrained power. Even when provoked, the great bear usually shows a placid nature. Although explorer Henry Kelsey declared in 1691 that "[the grizzly] is man's food and he makes food of man," grizzly attacks on humans are rare. According to biologist Stephen Herrero, quoted in *Wild Hunters: Predators in Peril*, "studies have shown that, even where grizzly bears have been shot and wounded, about three-quarters of the time they just try to get out of the way or go into cover."

Statistically, the chance of a grizzly attacking a human is very slight. In the last hundred years, less than forty people in North America have lost their lives from grizzly attacks. In the lower forty-eight U.S. states, only fourteen people have died from grizzly attacks since 1900. Alaska has recorded only twenty-four fatalities from bear attacks since the turn of the century. As grizzly guru Doug Peacock notes in *Grizzly Years*, "more people die of bad egg salad in a year than from grizzly attacks in a century."

The problem is that each attack spawns a mass of sensational media coverage, which only intensifies the grizzly's already bad press. You never hear about the six hundred people who die from hypothermia each year, but let one grizzly attack occur, and it's front page news. The paranoia that accompanies a bear attack is both amazing and appalling. When one resident of Naknek, Alaska, was mauled in the early 1970s by a female

(Above) Bear warning sign on a hiking trail.
(Opposite) This grizzly has lost a canine tooth, perhaps during a fight with another bear.

grizzly protecting her two cubs, furious townsfolk killed over a dozen innocent grizzlies in revenge. Not one person was charged by authorities.

Unfortunately, this paranoia has also carried over to affect the reintroduction efforts currently under way in parts of the United States. When the U.S. Fish and Wildlife Service announced plans in 1991 to relocate five or six grizzlies per year from southeast British Columbia to the Selway-Bitterroot area of central Idaho, there was a howl of protest from some local residents. One citizen wrote to the local paper, "As soon as they move more grizzlies in here, that's the last time I'm ever going into the woods." (Conservationists have been equally unhappy with the proposal. The grizzly population in southern British Columbia is decreasing, making it a poor choice from which to draw grizzlies. And it is doubtful if a dozen grizzlies exist in the Selway-Bitterroot area today; even at over a million acres, there is probably too much human activity in the area to accommodate a higher grizzly population.)

One of the worst problems in grizzly country today is the sloppy security around most rural garbage dumps. The B.C. Wildlife Branch states that "the majority of all bear attacks on humans in North America have been by bears that had fed on garbage or on other food sources such as orchards and compost heaps." In his classic *Bear Attacks: Their Causes and Avoidance*, Stephen Herrero stated: "Up to 1970, I calculated that inside the national parks, habituated, food-conditioned grizzlies were responsible for approximately two-thirds of all injuries inflicted on people." The key phrase here is "food-conditioned." Two decades of experience at McNeil River State Game Sanctuary in

Alaska have shown that grizzlies and humans can tolerate each other very well if the grizzlies have not learned to associate humans with easy food. Despite hundreds of human-bear encounters as close as eight feet, not one human has ever been harmed by a bear at McNeil River since the sanctuary was formed.

Grizzly problems often start when their territorial instinct breaks down in the face of excessive food left by sloppy humans. Unusual numbers of bears can be attracted to a single dump if the dump is not fenced or if it does not use bear-proof containers. At the old Lake Louise dump in Alberta, I have counted as many as seventeen of the great bears. (Rangers tell me they once counted twenty-three grizzlies at the dump.)

The most famous of all garbage-eating grizzlies were those at the Yellowstone National Park dumps during the 1960s. Adolph Murie in *A Naturalist in Alaska* wrote that he had seen in a Yellowstone garbage dump "thirty grizzlies wallowing together with bodies practically touching." Add one brain-dead tourist, and the combination spells bear attack.

For decades, tourists flocked to Yellowstone's garbage dumps to watch and photograph the great bears. Park rangers actually encouraged the feeding. In the February 1972 issue of *National Parks and Conservation* magazine, A. S. Johnson recounts: "Bleacher seats were built; lights were furnished; garbage was even sorted for bears. One retired park employee recalls the distribution of edible garbage on 'tables,' that visitors might have a better view of the bears as they fed." However, it finally became clear to park authorities that the attraction was creating dozens of bears that had lost their fear of humans.

John and Frank Craighead, two biologists who had studied the park's bears since the 1950s, recommended phasing out the dumps over a ten-year period, fearing that a rapid closing would cause the bears to stray widely in a desperate search for more garbage to feed upon. They foresaw increased numbers of incidents of bears entering public campgrounds. And increased numbers of grizzlies being shot.

However, park authorities disagreed and began abruptly closing the dumps in 1968. The Craigheads' worst nightmare came true as dozens of bears strolled into villages outside the park and marauded park campgrounds. Some were shot outside the park by hunters and ranchers. Others were killed by park rangers who feared that campers would be attacked. Although the exact numbers will never be known, it is likely that over a hundred grizzlies lost their lives between 1968 and the last dump closure in 1971.

To make matters even worse, in Yellowstone and elsewhere, many park campsites were located beside scenic streams and ponds — a great place for camping, but also a perfect place for bears. To date, most parks have not rectified this oversight. (Glacier National Park is one exception, and is now enclosing campsites located in high-risk areas with tall chain-link fences.) Still, the chance of a grizzly mauling in a park is less than one in a million.

However rare, grizzly attacks on humans do occur. One of the best-documented of grizzly attacks happened in 1983 in Yellowstone National Park. On June 24, Roger May, a twenty-three-year-old from Wisconsin, and his friend, Ted Moore, checked into the Rainbow Point campground. The two maintained a clean camp and carefully stowed their eating utensils in their car that night.

At about 2:30 in the morning, their tent began to shake, and the two young men attributed it to a prank. But the shaking was no joke. The intruder was an adult grizzly, who for some reason bit through the tent wall and grabbed May's neck. May began to scream as blood gushed from his neck when the big bear pulled him. The force of the pull was so strong that their brand-new tent canvas ripped, and May was pulled through the hole. When Moore rushed outside, the bear changed his grip to May's ankle and pulled him about thirty feet away. Moore looked around for a weapon and threw an aluminum tent pole at the bear, which moved off a few feet. At this point, Roger May was still alive — barely. But while his friend rummaged around inside the collapsed tent to find his glasses, the bear returned to May and pulled him off into the bushes.

By this time, other campers had arrived and chaos ensued as the hysterical group wandered about in the darkness trying to find May's body. Someone called the sheriff in West Yellowstone, and dozens of people combed the campground area all night long by flashlight. All this time, the grizzly was bedded down in thick brush only a short distance away, feeding upon Roger May.

The next morning, the Rainbow Point and nearby Bakers Hole campgrounds were evacuated. All trails in western Yellowstone were closed, and investigators on the ground and in helicopters searched the area. Thirteen bear traps were set, and late that night a large male grizzly was captured. The

(Opposite) A grazing grizzly looks far from vicious.

animal was tranquilized, and scrapings from its claws and muzzle were taken. Bear scat was collected from around the trap and sent to a lab in Missoula, Montana, for analysis, where it was determined that human hair found in the scat matched that of the victim. The bear was killed by a lethal injection.

Markings on the bear showed that it was bear Number 15, so-called because it had been the fifteenth bear caught and marked by the Interagency Grizzly Bear Study Team, a group formed in the early 1970s to undertake one of the most comprehensive grizzly studies ever. Although an autopsy found that the bear was in good physical condition, further studies found that the bear had been caught many times at or near garbage dumps in the twelve years it had been studied. Over this period it had gradually lost its fear of humans, and for this Roger May paid the ultimate price.

He was the first person killed by a grizzly in Yellowstone in over ten years.

In most fatal encounters between grizzlies and humans, the grizzly is simply reacting defensively. For example, a human might accidentally come between a mother and her cub, happen upon a grizzly lying beside its kill, or just stumble on a bear napping in its day bed. Actual intentional predation by grizzlies upon humans is extremely rare. However, studies of human injuries or deaths caused by black bears show that most have been the result of predation. Between 1978 and 1994, there were twenty-seven attacks on people by grizzlies in British Columbia, resulting in two deaths. During the same period, black bears attacked seventy-one people, resulting in nine deaths.

An Alaska guide once gave the following advice for those who stumble upon a grizzly in a park or other wild area: "Give it the opportunity to make a dignified retreat. Talk quietly to it. Don't look in its eyes. It might back off." And if it doesn't? "Then you're in big trouble."

Frank Dufresne, a former director of the Alaska Game Commission, believed that only one grizzly in twenty-five would charge. British Columbia bear hunter James Gary Shelton has had about fifty close encounters with grizzlies; half of the bears ran away, and half acted aggressively.

Experience shows, however, that most grizzlies do not begin to lick their chops when they spot human intruders in their territory. Most will flee. Most are long gone by the time the unsuspecting hiker or hunter blunders into their range.

Which are the most dangerous grizzlies? Studies show that females with cubs are probably at the top of the list. One research study found that in a bear population where only 17 percent of the animals were females with cubs, almost 80 percent of the human injuries caused by bears were caused by those females. In Stephen Herrero's exhaustive study of 279 grizzly–human encounters, 74 percent involved female grizzlies with cubs. He has postulated that the surly attitude of mothers with cubs arose as a behavioral adaptation to the current relatively open habitat in North America compared to

(Above) Black bears killed nine people in British Columbia between 1978 and 1994. (Opposite) Sitting in a cool pond is a good way to cool off at midday.

(Opposite) Blondie having a
good scratch in a meadow
above the Mansell River.

the thick protective forests of the grizzly's ancestral home in Asia.

Subadult bears, stressed by being driven off by their mothers, and not yet having learned to fear humans, are also often trouble bears. Like most teenagers, they tend to be both fearless and reckless. Half of all the fatal maulings in Glacier National Park have been by subadult grizzlies.

Statistically, September seems to be the worst month for grizzly attacks. Grizzlies in the fall must eat huge volumes of food in preparation for winter, and the desperate search for food seems to make bears incautious and aggressive. Half of all the fatal maulings of humans by grizzlies in Glacier National Park in the past thirty years have occurred in September.

September 1995 was a particularly bad month. In the first part of the month, a Helena, Montana, man named Lester Ashwood was mauled by a grizzly in Glacier National Park. On September 19, eighteen-year-old Bram Schaffer was badly mauled by a big female grizzly about ten miles north of Yellowstone National Park. About a week later, another big female grizzly marauded a campground at Lake Louise in Alberta, mauling six tourists.

There is also some evidence that the smell of human blood, detectable by bears in menstruating women, may attract curious bears, although some grizzly biologists do not believe this has been well documented. The smell of perfumes and colognes might similarly cause curious grizzlies to approach humans closer than they normally would. Lightning and thunder storms may also disturb bears and cause unnatural behavior. (Other animals may also be affected by nature's pyrotechnics. In 1994, I was trapped in a canoe in Cariboo Lake in central British Columbia on a wild stormy afternoon. The canoe had been pushed into the marsh at the north end of the lake by gale-force winds and three-foot-high waves and I was powerless to move the craft. Not fifty feet away, a young moose crashed through the willows, charging bushes and thrashing them with his antlers in fear. I often wonder what would have happened if I had been in his way.)

In August 1967, on the famous "Night of the Grizzlies," when two young women were killed by two different grizzlies at Trout Lake and Granite Park Campground in Glacier National Park, a number of tragic factors came into play. Firstly, the summer of 1967 was unusually hot and dry, with over a hundred lightning strikes in the park, which may have agitated the bears. The hot weather resulted in a poor berry crop and the bears soon learned to steal food from fishing camps and garbage dumps. Secondly, the situation in the park had been poorly managed. For three months prior to the fatal mauling of the young woman near Trout Lake, fishermen and hikers had lodged dozens of complaints about a very thin, unusually aggressive grizzly. Their complaints were ignored.

In the case of the young woman mauled in the Granite Park Campground, several more serious errors were made by park employees. Employees for months had been hauling garbage out to an open pit behind the Granite Park Chalet, where foraging grizzlies each night became quite a tourist attraction. This was a blatant violation of park policy, which dictated that garbage had to be either packed out or completely burned, but

like many rules, this one simply was not followed. The campground was located smack in the middle of an area frequented by grizzlies for at least ten years, and yet few people recognized the dangers. Worse yet, the Granite Park Campground was less than two hundred yards from the garbage dump itself.

After the Granite Park Campground mauling, park wardens were dispatched into the area with orders to kill every grizzly on sight, a heavy-handed procedure that resulted in the shootings of three grizzlies. Autopsies of the three bears showed that none was responsible for the mauling. Tragically, one of the bears was a mother with two cubs. A park official tried to shoot one of the cubs and succeeded in only wounding it, blowing away part of its jaw. Unbelievably, although both orphaned cubs stayed around the area for a long time, little effort was put into catching them or ending their suffering. A year later the wounded cub was spotted and seen to be in poor condition as it could not feed properly. A park ranger finally put the poor animal out of its misery. The fate of the other cub is unknown. The bear responsible for the fatal mauling at the Granite Park Campground was never positively identified.

After the two maulings, Glacier National Park officials instituted a long list of commonsense measures to prevent further bear–human problems. Trails were closed down at the first report of grizzlies in the area. Open garbage dumps were closed, and rangers enforced a strict "pack in, pack out" garbage policy with hikers and fishermen. Information booklets were distributed to educate back-country users. And all problem bears that bothered a human more than once were shot immediately.

Common sense in bear country is obviously the best solution to avoiding bear problems. Indians learned this a long time ago: Alaska's Koyukon Indians call the great bear *bik'ints'itldaadla*, meaning "keep out of its way."

A friendly argument.

Five

BACK AT THE BAR

(Above) A spawning salmon struggles up a waterfall.
(Opposite) A blue heron at sunrise.

BACK AT THE SALMON BAR, I DID TRY TO STAY OUT OF THE GREAT bears' way as much as possible. Sometimes I played with the idea of creeping closer but common sense prevailed.

It wasn't unusual to be serenaded by wild birds as I sat perched in my blind. Chickadees would scream their searching *Peter! Peter!* and glossy black ravens would add a gargly *Haa! Haa!* The chickadees often beat me to the blinds in the morning, sitting fluffed up in the frigid air like black-capped Easter chicks.

Both the mountain and the black-capped chickadee visited me at the blinds, the former distinguishable by its slighter build and a slash of white above the eye. One of my bird books stated that the two were never found together in the same habitat, but there they were, sitting happily side by side. Perhaps they hadn't read the book.

Other birds amused me not with song, but with acrobatics. Sandpipers sauntered along the riverbank, rhythmically bobbing up and down as if their legs were coil springs. Whiskeyjacks dashed drunkenly through the branches, hoping for a handout.

Once I spotted a great gray owl, sitting smug and inscrutable like a feathered Cheshire cat. Another time an evening grosbeak appeared in a flashy coat of bumblebee-yellow and raven-black. An impossibly large woodpecker once flew a slalom course through the woods around me — a pileated woodpecker, the largest woodpecker in North America with the demise of its ivory-billed cousins down south. Nuthatches would run straight up and down the tree trunk, a vertical highway that I could not travel unaided. And tiny hummingbirds, dressed in incredible Day-Glo colors, would sometimes appear in my blind, attracted by the red laces of my boots.

Along the trail to the bar, grouse would often explode underfoot, giving my heart an unwelcome early-morning jolt. Their eager drumming could often be heard close by in the woods, although I was seldom able to find the birds responsible.

By far the most colorful residents of the Mansell Valley are the butterflies, which seem attracted to the mudflats along the river. I have seen dozens of butterflies gathered at certain spots, which must be rich in salts or minerals. I have also seen Canada jays, or whiskeyjacks, take advantage of these gatherings and fly off with beaks full of quivering butterflies frantically flapping their last. Sometimes it looked like the butterflies were the ones carrying the bird away.

The whiskeyjacks are incredibly adept at finding food in the forest. If you're out on a hike or cross-country skiing and stop for a quick lunch, the birds appear out of nowhere to ask for a handout. There must be some kind of a bush telegraph that spreads the word, unheard by human ears. Their strange nickname is derived from the Algonquin Indian word *Wisakedjak*, the name of a mythical being who could assume any shape. And indeed when they do mysteriously materialize from nowhere, it does seem almost supernatural.

The valley contains many predators, and even the big jays have to watch themselves. I saw one disappear clutched in the talons of a red-tailed hawk, the most common raptor in the valley. And the hawk, in turn, is an occasional snack for the golden eagles, which drift like smoke high among the clouds. For some reason, the only eagle I have seen feeding on dead salmon is the bald eagle, although its golden cousin abounds in the valley. The golden eagle seems to be the better hunter and has plenty of mice, gophers, squirrels, and marmots to feed upon. The bald eagle, on the other hand, seems to be predominantly a scavenger. After years of lakeside living, I can only remember seeing a bald eagle catch a live fish once.

The two big birds also differ in their nesting sites. Bald eagles prefer to nest within fifty feet or so of lakes and rivers, usually in very tall trees. Golden eagles, at least in the Mansell area, like to nest on cliff edges. I once spent an afternoon looking for the nest of a golden eagle high up along the mountain cliffs overlooking the valley. It was a whole different world up there, steeped in the Pleistocene silence of ice and rock. Although I spotted what looked like a nest on a jutting ledge, there was no way I could reach it without climbing gear or riding on the back of a mountain goat.

Scraggly V-shaped flocks of Canada geese increasingly etched the sky as the fall season approached. Occasionally they would drop down to the marshes for

(Above) Butterflies add a splash of color to the mudflats. **(Opposite)** Bald eagles compete with bears for a fish dinner.

a day or two of feeding. Once they landed on the Salmon Bar and left a flood of hieroglyphic footprints in the soft mud. A few of the birds tentatively pecked at the rust-colored salmon eggs that sometimes washed up, but others avidly gobbled up the eggs, probably thinking them to be some kind of strange berry.

On one cold drizzly day, as the rain hissed through the trees and then fell plinking softly into the river, I waited for the bears to appear by watching a kingfisher. His claim to the river was in a side tributary, where a skinny brooklet gurgled over the rocks. Always on the same branch, the cheeky bird would spot a bite-sized fish, launch itself into the air, hover over the spot, and then execute a perfect dive into the rolling water. A quick flip of the head and a two-inch minnow would be history. Then a staccato call, *ca-ca-ca-ca*-ing its joy at being alive on the river, and back to its perch on the cedar.

Those lovely cedars. Their deeply incised trunks, with long strips of shaggy brown bark, made the trees look like they had been sunburned and were now peeling. The intricately laced leaves looked as though they had been woven together by some loving hand. All filled with a lifesaving oil that prevents the tree from drying out in times of drought. I once took an armful of cedar boughs back to my house, where I placed them in a vase of water on the kitchen table. They lasted, rich, green and fragrant, for over a month.

Occasionally, other animals besides grizzlies would come down to the river for a feed. Bald eagles were the most numerous of these, parked on treetops awaiting a chance to swoop down and grab a morsel or two. I once saw an eagle steal a fish from an osprey, another riverside raptor in the Mansell Valley. The majestic eagle, symbol of America, stealing food from a little fish hawk. Another false god crashes to the ground.

Sometimes a family of otters would appear in the early morning, rolling and cavorting in the shallows like a troupe of slick-furred acrobats. I often saw fat porcupines waddling through the woods, full of confidence in their coats of quills. And once a beautiful red fox sauntered onto the bar, checked out the competition, and wisely decided to leave the bar to the bears.

The hyperactive squirrels were omnipresent — pint-sized wardens of the woods scolding intruders of all sizes. I was once amused to see a squirrel tugging at one corner of a towel that I kept on hand to soften my folding chair; it was probably hoping to use it for den-lining material. The little devil dragged it off about a foot before I retrieved it, receiving a royal scolding for my efforts.

One afternoon two scrawny coyotes appeared at the edge of the meadow above the gravel bar. As loon is to lake, coyote is to country; one of the best-adapted of animals, coyotes can be found from parched deserts to lush mountain valleys. Both these coyotes looked like they could use a good feed, and I suspect they had traveled far from their normal stomping grounds in search of food.

(Above) A porcupine, confident in his coat of quills. (Opposite) A squirrel perched on aspen fungus.

They were obviously attracted by the tempting aroma of dead fish, but hesitated when they saw that all the tables were taken by huge grizzlies. Still, the coyote has survived because of its renowned wits, and these two were not to go hungry that day.

Ignoring all the other bears, they chose Grumpy as their target and minced softly in his direction. As soon as Grumpy saw them, their gait changed, and they began dancing around like whirling dustdevils. I began to wonder if they had rabies when one danced close to Grumpy and he charged it with a roar. Immediately, the other coyote dashed in, grabbed Grumpy's fish, and ran off into the woods. His partner easily evaded Grumpy and followed. I had to smile. I wonder if they chose Grumpy because he looked less sharp than the other bears, sitting in the shallows like some big dummy?

A bough of cedar — fresh, green, and fragrant.

The only other interspecies action I ever observed with the grizzlies I almost missed due to the Terror Twins.

I had been watching the Twins playing at one end of the bar, rearing on their hind legs and jabbing at each other with their front paws, like two small, hairy boxers. Out of the corner of my eye, I suddenly noticed a large shape at the other end of the bar: a cow moose and her calf. Behind them was a grizzly, a subadult who had obviously chased them out of the bush. A female moose can do a very good job of protecting her young, and this one was no exception. The calf stood glued to her side, and she turned to face the young grizzly head on.

Each time he charged, she kicked out a sharp hoof, connecting once with the bear's shoulder. The slashing punch must have been extremely painful, but the young grizzly didn't know when to quit. None of the other bears on the bar entered the fray. If these had been wolves, a communal effort would have probably brought down the calf, but bears are individual hunters. Although the other bears seemed to watch with interest, none participated, and the Terror Twins played on, oblivious to the action at the other end of the bar. The young grizzly kept charging in and then backing off when faced with the hard flying hooves of momma moose.

This went on for about five minutes until finally the moose took control of the situation and charged the young grizzly. He ran off about fifty feet and seemed to reevaluate his chances. Then he took one final look at the moose and ran back to the river, where the dying salmon made an easier meal that couldn't fight back. Incredibly, the mother moose charged him as soon as his back was turned, as if to say *and don't you try it again*. She then calmly climbed up into the brush, her calf madly scrambling behind her, and trotted away.

The moose is the largest animal in the Mansell Valley. I often surprised moose along the riverbanks as I made my way to the camera blinds each morning, and their initial reaction was usually one of shock at seeing a human in their woods. Like many animals, the moose

A Canada goose nest.

**Canada goose tracks
in river sand.**

is the subject of many a campfire tale, most of which are long on fantasy and short on fact.

One of my neighbors used to be a hunting guide, a man who spent many years chasing game as a "professional." And yet this man believes so many fantasies about wildlife that I sometimes wonder what kind of stuff he smokes in his pipe. He once told me, straight-faced, that he had seen moose calves hide from hunters by jumping into lakes and holding their breaths underwater. He also thinks that moose calves cross large lakes by hitching a ride on the backs of their mothers.

I don't believe either tale, but I have witnessed a mother moose and calf swim two miles across an icy mountain lake and emerge undaunted to charge off into the bush. And many times when I have been out canoeing I have seen a moose swimming in the lake and have attempted unsuccessfully to keep up with it. Their strength and stamina are simply amazing.

It's hard to believe that such a large animal can be such a good swimmer, especially with such skinny-looking legs. But perhaps it is the huge dish-shaped feet that actually do much of the paddling.

(Above) Cow moose and calf swimming across a lake. (Opposite) A pair of spawning sockeyes in the shallows.

The river itself showed many faces in the short stretch that was visible from my blinds. Just south of the bar, beside a fallen cedar, was a small whirlpool, where bright orange leaves floated round and round in a spiral ballet. Below the small rapid above the bar was a smooth section of absolutely flat water; it looked like it had been chromed and polished. Only a few feet away, a rocky riverbed created a choppy section of angry angular waves. Beneath it all lay the salmon.

On days when nothing much was happening in the bear world, I often spent hours staring at the water, giving in to the primal attraction between man and that magic fluid, and watching the tragic drama of spawning sockeyes.

The sockeye salmon begins life as a rust-colored egg, buried lovingly under protective gravels at the bottom of a number of ice-cold rivers. And not just any gravel will do: it has to be the right size to allow the circulation of water over the precious eggs. Sockeyes tend to prefer gravel a half to four and a half inches in diameter.

Eighty-five percent of sockeye eggs never hatch. Some are eaten by trout, ducks, herons, or otters. Some are washed away by fall floods and die. Some freeze in unusually cold winters. Some die when unusually warm winters result in low spring water levels, which cause warmer water than that required to hatch eggs. But some do hatch into tiny fish called alevins, which at first hide among the rocks, living off their attached eggsacs. The young fish stay in their home river and surrounding lakes for one or two years, during which time two out of three will die from predation.

The survivors then head seaward, swimming down the Fraser River to the sea, where they begin a long lazy loop along the coast, first heading north to Alaskan waters, then west toward Japan, and finally back toward the mouth of the Fraser. Their time at sea may range

from two to four years. When they reach adulthood, instinct tells them to return to the rivers of their birth. This is no easy task.

Biologists are still unsure how the fish find the right streams and right patches of riverbeds. Some think it is genetically encoded in young fish. Others believe the fish use taste or smell or magnetic fields to distinguish their home waters. Humans have played

A spawned-out salmon.

havoc with these returning fish both by overfishing and by polluting the waters with runoff due to clear-cutting, pesticides from agricultural use, and waste disposal from riverside pulp and paper plants. And if the fish manage to avoid the vast array of nets and traps that await them, they still face a final 550-mile pilgrimage to their home gravels. It is a miracle that any fish find their way home at all. So difficult is the life of the salmon that for every four thousand eggs, only two will survive to reach adulthood, migrate, and spawn.

The sockeyes are beaten and battered by the time they reach their spawning grounds. In fact, the time of spawning marks a time of rapid deterioration of their bodies. Their pituitary and adrenal glands speed up their activities and the fish literally begin to fall apart. Spawning salmon also often suffer from hardening of the arteries, just like aging humans. Their bodies are cut and bruised, and white wisps of slimy fungus sprout from infected areas. I once found a female sockeye in a lake many miles downstream of the Mansell River

gravels. Both of her eyes were completely covered with fungus, and the bedraggled fish was swimming in circles, trying to find the river mouth at the end of the lake. I netted her and took her there myself, crossing my fingers as she laboriously swam away.

The male sockeyes are especially fierce during the spawning season, chasing away smaller males and spreading out all their fins in order to look as large and awesome as possible. Sometimes they even tear chunks of flesh out of other males, making the action in a human singles bar look tame in comparison. To stimulate the females, the males slide over their backs, or hover over them and quiver, sending vibrations into the water that seem to excite the females.

Female sockeyes are picky about choosing nest sites and prefer well-aerated sites in front of logs or rocks. Once they've chosen a site, the females roll on their sides and excavate a shallow nest by slapping their tails against the river bottom. The average sockeye nest is an oval scoop over three feet long and three and a half inches deep. Big chinook salmon dig such deep nests that piles of gravel three feet high may heap up at the end of the nest. The low spots between these piles are favorite resting spots for trout and other fish.

Each female lays from 2,500 to 4,500 eggs in her nest, which may be fertilized by more than one male. The male releases his sperm with an orgasmic quiver, and when all his sperm is exhausted, he will die. The females guard their nests and add bits of gravel to the nest sites until death takes its final hold. For the average female sockeye, only nine to ten days exist between the time she lays her first eggs and the time she dies.

I noticed that fish near death often stayed in the

Grumpy looking for fish in the shallows of the Mansell River.

part of the river where the current was the strongest, pushing life-giving oxygen over their failing gills. Even hours away from death, the pulse of life still tries valiantly to beat on.

After she dies, a female's body joins the rest of the carcasses rocking slowly in the rhythmic wake of the Mansell River, providing food for many a grizzly. Like other events in nature, the arrival of the salmon is carefully timed. In midsummer, the protein content of some grasses and sedges approaches 25 percent. A few months later, when the vivid greens turn to dying browns, the protein drops to 5 percent or less. Just when this happens, and when the bears need protein the most prior to denning, the salmon arrive on the scene. Nature's timing couldn't be better.

I was often struck by the thought that I was incredibly lucky to have the chance to watch grizzlies and the other riverside residents going about their day-to-day lives. How sad that our education system emphasizes the insides of animals — and dead animals at that. How much more exciting are the everyday lives of living creatures. I remember the day we had to dissect a frog in school, a day of horror for all concerned. What did that teach us, compared to what we would have learned in the field, watching the magical transformation of tadpole to frog, of frog stalking bug, of frog evading the quick red fox? The only field trip that I can remember from all those years of grade school was a trip to the local sewage treatment plant. I don't remember learning anything from the trip.

Occasionally, unusually warm September days would put a damper on activities at the Salmon Bar. Studies have shown that there is little grizzly activity when temperatures are above 72°F. Most of the bears did very little fishing on those days, preferring to lie in the cool shade of the riverbank or not emerging from the woods at all. The exception was the Terror Twins.

On one hot day, when all the bears were bedded down and the bar was quiet, the Twins found a gopher. The little rodent had a burrow at one end of the bar and had, probably wisely, not appeared until now. As soon as the cubs spotted the gopher, they forgot about being primarily vegetarians and launched a pursuit. With mighty bounds, the two little bears chased the gopher from one end of the bar to the other. Their coordination, however, couldn't quite match the gopher's, and by the time the gopher had already darted off in another direction, the cubs were falling over themselves to stop. I got the distinct impression that the gopher wasn't really trying. After a few minutes it tired of the game and zipped down its burrow. The cubs didn't see the gopher go and spent almost five minutes sniffing over the entire bar looking for it. And the score is gopher one, cubs zero, but richer in learning a little more about hunting.

Although the Twins were the ones who played the most, even the big adult grizzlies played together on occasion. (Other authors have observed grizzlies sliding down snow banks, playing with sticks, and gleefully tossing about floating logs — behavior that would shock those who still believe that the big bear is the most vicious bully in the forest.) At the Salmon Bar, two subadults could often be seen standing on their hind legs and tussling, testing each other's strength and stamina. Perhaps the winner would gain a choicer

(Left) Subadult grizzlies often wrestle along the riverbanks. (Above) Ravens are among the most playful and intelligent of birds.

fishing spot; these young bears looked so much alike that I had problems identifying them.

I also had problems taking pictures of the bears actually feeding, for they tended to feed late at night, after most of the light had gone. Like most nature photographers, I missed a lot of great shots. One of the worst misses happened after a day of pouring rain. I noticed a bear sniffing around in the rushes at the edge of the river and couldn't figure out what he was after. Then he turned my way, with a drowned baby bird in his mouth. Apparently a nest in the rushes had fallen into the water, and the bear had snapped up the dead birds.

Although I missed that shot due to the heavy mist after the rain, I did get one shot as a result of a simple experiment. In order to test the great bears' sense of smell, one morning I hid four salmon under a pile of brush and logs on a small sand bar downstream. Although the bar was a quarter-mile from the bears' usual feeding spot, two grizzlies were there within a half hour. One was so filled with fish that he lazily draped himself over a log after gorging himself, looking like a spaced-out cat after a feed of catnip.

On another unusually hot September day I went swimming in the Mansell River marshes, a few miles downstream from the Salmon Bar. There the river looped around like a writhing snake, and some of the shallower loops were warm enough to swim in.

After paddling around for a few minutes, I noticed that I had company. Where a side stream entered the marsh, some creature was porpoising through the water in a series of effortless dives. When it stopped and

(Above) River otters are common in the Mansell River; this one's gray face suggests an advanced age. (Opposite) A river otter shoots through a sun-splashed pond.

treaded water with its head toward me, I saw what it was: a river otter, a common resident in the Mansell River.

The otter had spotted me and was watching me closely, probably trying to figure out just what type of animal I was. In all likelihood, it had never seen a human before. And since I only had my head showing, I probably didn't look too large or dangerous.

After about ten seconds of scrutiny, the otter chittered a few notes like an angry squirrel, then dove underwater in a smooth rolling motion and promptly reappeared on the surface with a small fish held in its paws. I couldn't believe how fast it had happened; the otter must have grabbed the fish within seconds. It then sat there treading water munching on the fish, turning it in its paws like a cob of corn. From twenty feet away I could hear the crunch of snapping fish bones. I swam away quietly and left the otter to his noisy lunch.

Devil's club, the nemesis of hikers.

One warm Saturday morning I backtracked along the trail the bears used from the woods onto the bar. I soon found that in places the trail had been trodden three inches into the ground. How long had those bears been using the trail? Years? Decades? I remember watching the tragic sight of a zoo bear pacing back and forth, back and forth, along one wall of its cage. No stresses, no changes, no joys, just back and forth. It, too, had worn a path in the concrete floor of its cage, but it was a path of anguish.

The trail in the woods led through a thick patch of willows for about 150 feet. Suspended in one willow I found a perfect robin's nest, complete with three china blue eggs, tiny seeds of the sky. What had led the mother robin to vacate her nest, to break the strongest of bonds? I left the tiny birds-that-would-never-be and trudged on.

Soon the trail meandered through a grove of huge cedars where godbeams of light stabbed through at intervals. I was reminded of a painting by Emily Carr, which she described as "green jungle . . . with a helter-skelter magnificence." Few other artists have felt the ordered chaos of the woods, and fewer still have reproduced it so vividly.

Beyond the cedars, a patch of poplars stood knee deep in devil's club, the nemesis of hikers everywhere. Their leaves are like elephants' ears, some measuring a foot in diameter. But the underside of the leaves is covered in thorns, as is the bamboo-like stem. The plants grabbed at my legs, clutched at my boot-laces, and impaled my hands more than once. How much better adapted were the great bears, which plowed through this patch daily. No thorn would catch their thick coats, and their leathery footpads would repel all but the sharpest of stones or quills.

Emerging from the poplar stand, I surprised a tawny doe and her two late-season fawns. One fawn crashed off into the woods, but the other flattened itself on the ground, front legs outstretched and chin in the dirt. In the world of the wild, this would have been

(Left) The soaring firs, straight out of an Emily Carr painting. (Above) A rare shot of a pair of lynx, which usually stay together only during the mating season in March–April.

(Above) Wasp nests become visible in the fall. (Right) Poplars are a favorite food of beavers along the Mansell River.

the fawn taken by a predator, the one whose defense had not worked. I backed off about a hundred feet, and after a few minutes the fawn got up and trotted off in the direction of its mother. In the direction of life.

The trail wandered higher and higher until it ended at a rock scree at the base of a mountain where a half-dozen hoary marmots squealed their indignation at my intrusion. With their fat bellies distended with grasses and leaves, they reminded me of children's roly-poly toys, the ones you push over only to have them pop back up again. To the bears, of course, the marmots were chubby chunks of protein, an important part of their fall diet.

Beyond the talus were the mountains, massive crags that stared down upon me with stony indifference. Had humans ever penetrated farther into their wilderness? Or more importantly, should they? Some lands should never be trodden. It was discovered a few years ago that wolves on the isolated island of Isle Royale in Lake Superior have been infected with distemper, thought to have been borne in on a visitor's boots. How subtle the damage humans can unknowingly bring, but how tragic the consequences. I stared at the purest wilderness that I have ever seen, and then began the long hike home. The mountains could keep their secrets a while longer.

Toward the end of September, the days were getting short and the number of hours of daylight suitable for bear-watching became fewer. I decided to improve my odds by purchasing a grizzly call at a big city hunting shop. The store made my skin crawl, with stuffed animals on every wall staring at me with glazed eyes. I felt guilty about giving business to such a place and even sicker when I heard one Rambo wanna-be at the counter talk about spotting a wolf, declaring with a vocal swagger that he would "sure like to shoot one of those damn things."

Had he ever watched a mother wolf play with her young? Or seen a pack of wolves bring food back to feed an injured comrade? The thought of shooting one of these awesome animals and hanging it up on the wall was abhorrent. I closed my eyes, made my purchase, and retreated from the little shop of horrors.

The next day at the Salmon Bar I tried the Benco Grizzly Call, guaranteed for "grizzlies large and small." However, I wasn't quite prepared for what I heard. It sounded like an old cow with a severe case of asthma. Maybe I wasn't blowing it right. I doubted that even a horny male grizzly in breeding season would find it appealing, unless he was *really* desperate. I tried again, giving the thing a mighty, lung-sapping burst of air. Two grizzlies looked up and then ran away. I never did get my money back from Benco.

Marmots constitute important sources of fall protein for the Mansell bears.

Late September is one of my favorite times of the year, for when all the leaves have fallen, a whole new world opens up to the naturalist. Wasp and bird nests become visible for the first time without the dense cover of foliage. I often took photos of unusual nests, and then ran home to look them up in my bird books, discovering whole new inhabitants of my well-trodden woods. Woodpecker and owl holes could similarly be spotted. I marked their locations on detailed topo sheets so that I could return for photography in the summer.

This is the time when the beavers store twigs and branches in preparation for winter. Often I would arrive at the gravel bar only to find that half of my camera blind had been gnawed away. And small riverside aspens disappeared nightly, leaving foot-high stumps carefully chewed off by the beavers' giant incisors.

September is also the time when black bears descend to the valley bottoms for an orgy of feasting prior to hibernation. I never saw any blacks on the Salmon Bar — grizzlies often kill their smaller cousins — but a number of black bears did make the mistake of approaching the nearest townsite, where they were shot on sight. One Saturday I counted two black bear carcasses at the local dump and another a mile from town, where the bear had been shot while innocently crossing the road. That same afternoon two people told me about shooting other bears that they'd seen near town.

Why is this carnage allowed in a province that bills itelf as "Beautiful B.C."? Do politicians not understand that wildlife is as valuable a resource as their beloved timber stands? All life is precious, be it leaved or furred. Nuisance bears are one thing, and aggressive bears that challenge humans are another, but most bears shot in British Columbia are shot for no reason at all other than the fact that they are bears. Wildlife managers will tell you that the black bear population in British Columbia is large and stable, but this is no reason to sanctify witless slaughter. We must not be complacent about large populations; biologists once told us that the passenger pigeon and the buffalo were "safe" species. On a more local scale, it is also wise to remember that high numbers of grizzlies once roamed the townsite area. But no more. They were all shot out long ago. Humans are so slow to learn.

Six

OF BEARS AND MEN

AT ONE TIME, THE GRIZZLY ROAMED OVER MUCH OF NORTH America, never reaching the East Coast, but pushing as far as Minnesota, Kansas, and Nebraska in the United States and as far east as central Manitoba in Canada. The grizzly used to be abundant on the Canadian prairies; Hudson Bay Company records for 1871–72 show that 750 grizzly pelts were taken in just a few months in what is now southwest Saskatchewan. Ernest Thompson Seton wrote that in the Black Hills of South Dakota, great numbers of grizzlies traveled "in bands like buffalo" and were treated with great respect by the local natives.

It is not surprising that early native Indians both feared and revered the great grizzly. Some saw a grizzly kill as a badge of courage; one historian wrote, "the death of a bear gives the warrior greater renown than the scalp of a human enemy." Others held the bear in such awe that it was taboo to even mention its name.

Of course, sometimes the grizzly did not appreciate the reverence shown it by the local natives. Claude Jean Allouez, a European missionary to the Pacific Northwest, wrote in 1666 about a native Indian tribe who "live on raw fish; but these people, in turn, are eaten by bears of frightful size . . . with prodigiously long claws."

Anthropologist Richard Nelson wrote in *Make Prayers to the Raven* that among Alaska's Koyukon Indians, even the hide of a grizzly was a spiritual item: "It takes a few years for all that life to

(Above) Detail from *A Close Call*, William Robinson Leigh, 1914. *(Courtesy of Thomas Gilcrease Institute of American History & Art, Tulsa, Oklahoma)*
(Opposite) A trophy grizzly shot near Telegraph Creek, British Columbia. *(Photo: E. Whalley)*

be gone from a brown bear's hide. That's the kind of power it has."

The Shasta Indians thought that if a man sat down quietly and did not flee from a grizzly, it would sit down and speak with him. Haida Indians told their children the legend of the Bear Mother, in which a woman marries a grizzly and their children become the ancestors of all native Indians, giving them strength and the ability to survive in the wild. And California's Pomo Indians believed that good men went to Heaven after death, but that bad men stayed on Earth in the shape of a grizzly.

Natives in the Stikine region of British Columbia told the legend of a great flood crossing the land; the people who jumped into the water became seals and those who ran into the forests became grizzlies. British Columbia's Thompson Indians painted their faces black as a token of respect when they killed an enemy warrior or a grizzly.

Many other native tribes identified just as closely with grizzlies: the Sauk Indians called the grizzly "Old Man," the Cree called him "Chief's Son," and the Menominee knew him as "Elder Brother." Some tribes refused to eat grizzly flesh, for to do so would be tantamount to cannibalism. When explorer Henry Kelsey crossed the Canadian plains in 1690 and killed a grizzly, his native Indian companions were horrified. "It was a god," they said.

Such reverence did not last with the coming of the white man to North America. Grizzlies were first encountered by Spanish settlers in California, where the lush coastal forests once held great numbers of bears. In 1769, the first California grizzly killed by a

white man was recorded. It was the spark of a devastation that has seldom been equaled in the sad annals of wildlife in North America.

At first, the early settlers killed the grizzlies by roping them with strong lariats called "reatas." A roped grizzly was usually stabbed to death, but sometimes two riders roped opposite ends of a bear and literally pulled it apart. Even the Spanish priests joined in these cruel hunts; one account tells of a Father Réal, who "was often known to go with young men on moonlight rides, lassoing grizzly bears."

Early settlers in California often reported seeing fifty grizzlies in one day. One 1852 report stated that "schools [were] closed because [it was] unsafe for children to use trails." "Old Ephraim," as the grizzly was called, was everywhere. Grizzly steaks became a common food item.

The great bears soon came into conflict with humans who attempted with little effect to protect their livestock from the huge predators. That is, until 1848, when Sharps marketed the first breech-loaded rifle, replacing the clumsy old muzzle-loaders. This simple development, unheralded at first, spelled doom for the coastal grizzlies.

As humans gained mastery over the big bear through sheer firepower, fear gave rise to incredibly cruel "sports" that reeked of the bad old days of the Roman Colosseum. Bear-baiting was common sport during California's roaring gold-rush days. A cord twenty yards long was tied to the front hoof of a bull and the rear paw of a bear. The two were then released in a pen to fight to the death, while bloodthirsty humans watched and wagered. This type of inane duel

(Opposite) *Roping a Wild Grizzly,*
James Walker, 1877.
(Courtesy of Thomas Gilcrease
Institute of American History &
Art, Tulsa, Oklahoma)

lasted well into the end of the 1800s. (In a sad variation on the theme, in the 1920s one of the last California grizzlies was sent to Monterrey, Mexico, where it was set against an African lion. It was reported that the bear "killed him so quickly that the big audience hardly knew how it was done." The fate of the victorious bear was not mentioned.)

The new Sharps rifle allowed an unprecedented degree of slaughter. A number of early California hunters claimed to have each killed over two hundred grizzlies within a single year. In Oregon, five hunters emerged after a year of hunting in 1848 with seven hundred grizzly pelts. Within a hundred years of the invention of the Sharps rifle, the California grizzly had been hunted to extinction. The "golden bear," the very symbol of the state, was gone forever.

The rapid devastation of the California grizzly population was paralleled across the country. Whenever an explorer or settler met a bear, the animal usually paid for the meeting with its life. When Meriwether Lewis and John Clark trekked to the Missouri River in 1805, they spotted a grizzly and "immediately went to attack him," callously noting: "it is astonishing to see the wounds they will bear before they can be put to death." The documented dates of "last grizzly" killings follow the spread of settlers across the West: Texas 1890, North Dakota 1897, California 1922, Utah 1923, Oregon and New Mexico 1935, Arizona 1939.

Part of the problem was that in those early pre-conservation days, no one worried about the future of the great bear. Pioneer conservationist Aldo Leopold wrote in *A Sand County Almanac*: "In 1909, when I first saw the West, there were grizzlies in every major mountain pass, but you could travel for months without meeting a conservation officer."

Today, excluding Alaska, 99 percent of the original grizzly population in the United States is gone. There are perhaps 700 to 900 grizzlies left in the lower forty-

eight states: 350 to 650 in the Glacier National Park area of Montana, about 250 in the Yellowstone National Park ecosystem, and a dozen or so in each of the Bob Marshall Wilderness (Montana), North Cascade Mountains (Washington), Selkirk Mountains (Idaho), and Cabinet Mountains (Idaho-Montana).

Yellowstone's 250 bears sounds like a comfortable number. However, many think that the park may still

(Above) Ninety-nine percent of the original grizzly population in the mainland United States is gone. (Opposite) *A Wounded Grizzly,* **Charles M. Russell, 1906.** *(Courtesy of Whitney Gallery of Western Art, Cody, Wyoming)*

become an island of extinction. "The grizzly program is not a success story," says Louisa Willcox of the Greater Yellowstone Coalition. "We've gotten some problems under control, like garbage and public education, but that's the easy stuff. The hard stuff is meaningful habitat protection." A 1989 Montana State University study was more blunt: "The Yellowstone grizzly population is doomed to extinction."

A few other pockets of grizzly habitat may still exist. In 1979, a big game outfitter killed a sixteen-year-old female grizzly in the San Juan Mountains of Colorado. The man stated that he had been charged by the bear, and then stabbed it in the throat with an arrow. However, there was also an arrow wound in the bear's shoulder, leading many people to suspect that the bear had first been wounded. Even though the grizzly had been declared an endangered species in the lower forty-eight states in 1975, the man was not charged by authorities.

It is unlikely that the small clumps of grizzly habitat in Idaho, Washington, and perhaps Colorado will last much longer. Biologist Mark Shaffer, who wrote his doctoral thesis at Duke University on the Yellowstone grizzly, refers to the patches of remaining grizzly habitat as "an archipelago of isolated population remnants, none of which is sufficiently large to be viable in its own right." He found that under normal circumstances, once a grizzly population drops below fifty to ninety bears, that population is inevitably headed for extinction.

Alaska today harbors about forty thousand grizzlies. As huge as this number sounds, it is best to remember Aldo Leopold's famous comment from

A Sand County Almanac: "Relegating grizzlies to Alaska is about like relegating happiness to heaven; one may never get there."

Mexico's last grizzly was killed in 1960, although a number of grizzly reports continued in the mountainous state of Chihuahua through 1969, and the odd report surfaces even today.

Canada hasn't had quite such a bad record. As Thomas McNamee wrote in *The Grizzly Bear*: "Canadians seem never to have harried their varmints with quite the same addled glee as the Americans." In Canada, grizzlies still occupy half of their original range, with perhaps twenty thousand grizzlies surviving today. Their highest numbers are in British Columbia.

Quite predictably, the effect of humans on grizzlies is often negative. According to B.C. bear biologist Bruce McLellan, "The problem is not that grizzlies can't adapt to people, but that people can't adapt to grizzlies." Grizzlies can readily live alongside man with few problems, but trigger-happy humans often end the relationship with a bang. As McLellan says, "They're an extremely adaptable animal, but they're not adaptable to being shot."

Biologists have long tried to quantify how many bears can be safely taken from a given population without that population slowly decreasing to extinction. In 1991, the prestigious Committee on the Status of Endangered Wildlife in Canada recommended 4 percent as the maximum total harvest rate for any given grizzly population. (The B.C. Wildlife Branch also recommends the same figure.)

The Committee identified twelve Bear Zones where the great bear still existed in Canada. In almost half of the zones, studies of official statistics showed that the bear was being overhunted. Add to that the number of problem bears killed illegally and the number of poached bears, and the magnitude of the overkill swells to serious proportions.

British Columbia currently quotes ten thousand to thirteen thousand as the "official" provincial grizzly population. However, this number may well be high; a number of conservationists have suggested the actual population is closer to seven thousand. Veteran bear biologist Wayne McCrory believes it may even be as low as five to six thousand.

Government predator estimates often run high — bear permits bring in big bucks and the ties between wildlife departments and the hunting fraternity are close. (It could well be argued that for years wildlife departments existed primarily to serve hunters and not wildlife; it wasn't until 1974 that the first *non*game management course was offered in North America, at Colorado State University in Fort Collins. In many areas, it was not until the 1990s that trained wildlife biologists began to infiltrate the ranks of wildlife departments.) In British Columbia, the 1997 species license fee for a grizzly was $530 for nonresidents, the highest fee levied for any big game animal in the province. Residents had only to pay a paltry $80. In 1996, British Columbia made almost $3 million on grizzly hunting licenses. Of British Columbia's 5,000 to 13,000 grizzlies, an average of 350 per year are legally shot by resident and nonresident hunters. The number of legal kills has been generally declining since 1991. Another 50 grizzlies are killed annually as nuisance bears. (There are an estimated 200,000 black bears in British Columbia. An average of 4,000 are killed by hunters each year and 800 are killed as nuisance bears.)

The number of grizzlies killed illegally is a matter of much dispute. A 1991 study by biologist Vivian Banci found that illegal kills of grizzlies had been underestimated in every jurisdiction in western Canada. A 1989 internal B.C. Wildlife Branch memo leaked to the Western Canada Wilderness Committee revealed that the number of illegal and unreported kills of grizzlies was almost equal to the legal kill. Researchers Andrew Trites and Harvey Thommasen did a survey of grizzly deaths in the Bella Coola watershed between 1975 and 1988 and found that of eighty-nine grizzlies killed, fifty-seven were killed as nuisance bears or illegally killed. The official number of grizzlies killed in the area according to B.C. Wildlife Branch statistics was thirty-two, less than half the actual total. Add to that the number of poached bears that are never discovered, and the total provincial grizzly harvest may actually be as high as 10 percent of the grizzly population, more than twice the recommended harvest rate.

Since grizzly meat is not a common human food, most grizzlies that are legally shot are taken as trophies. An adult trophy grizzly may bring $10,000 on the black market; claws can go for $300 each and gall bladders for up to $2,000. In October 1995, a grizzly carcass was found near Quesnel, British Columbia, with only the

(Above) False solomon's seal, which loses its sensuous aroma by midsummer. (Opposite) The black bear is the most common bear in British Columbia.

penis bone missing. Ground up and used in potions, the bone is prized in Chinese medicine as an aphrodisiac. The incident sums up the shocking magnitude of the poaching problem: an entire grizzly killed just for one small bone destined to boost the love life of some elderly Asian. However, it is thought that the rarity of the grizzly has sheltered it somewhat from poachers compared to the thousands of black bears illegally killed each year. In addition, trophy hunting is growing in disfavor; according to a 1995 Angus Reid poll, 78 percent of British Columbians believe that trophy hunting is unacceptable and should be outlawed.

(Above) As a new day dawns, a coat of light creeps across the treetops. (Opposite) Habitat loss from clear-cutting is the most serious problem faced by grizzlies in British Columbia.

There is also some evidence that trophy hunting can have negative effects on grizzly populations. In a ten-year study by biologist Robert Wielgus, it was discovered that most trophy grizzlies are large males. The removal of these males was found to cause an increase in the number of cubs eaten by young male bears, who try to establish new harems by forcing the female grizzlies into heat again by killing their cubs. It was also found that in many cases, females moved their cubs into less choice, food-poor areas to avoid the threat of young male grizzlies, threatening the long-term viability of the whole grizzly population. Wielgus's study has been ignored by the B.C. Wildlife Branch, which has stated that the "recreational demand" for trophy grizzlies justifies the hunt.

One might think that sufficient numbers of grizzlies are protected in parks. However, the preservation of grizzlies and other large predators in parks and reserves cannot be guaranteed for the simple reason that animals do not respect political boundaries. A study of twelve resident grizzlies in British Columbia's Yoho National Park determined that when nine of these bears left the park, they were all shot within a year.

One answer to this tragic loss of life is to establish no-hunting buffer zones around such parks. This has been done recently in the case of the Khutzeymateen provincial park in northwest British Columbia. Another is to add additional reserves as refuges for grizzlies. And still another solution is to stop the legal hunting of grizzlies that is still allowed in some provincial parks.

An additional factor in grizzly management is the distressing number of grizzlies accidentally shot each year by hunters who mistook them for black bears. (One of the worst such incidents occurred in 1983, when hunters in northern Montana accidentally killed five grizzlies in ten days.) Improved hunter training is obviously in order. Furthermore, one Yukon study found that one grizzly in four shot by hunters was only wounded. Apparently, many hunters need to be taught *how* to shoot as well.

Like every other North American predator, the grizzly has suffered tremendously due to loss of habitat. In British Columbia, the most serious such threat is clearcut logging, which has left a checkerboard of destruction across the entire province. The B.C. Wildlife Branch admits, "Grizzly bear habitat management and

forestry have a long history of conflict in British Columbia."

Loggers are quick to point out that clear-cutting does provide some short-term benefits to grizzlies, such as the growth of new grasses and berry shrubs on clear-cut blocks. However, according to the B.C. Wildlife Branch, "most of the benefits associated with timber harvesting are negated by the intensive land use and management that follows."

A bear's eye view of a poplar in autumn.

Tony Hamilton, a B.C. Wildlife Branch bear biologist, believes that the provincial grizzly population is on the decline and that one of the most significant factors in the decline is logging. Over a thousand acres of B.C. forest are logged *every day*, most of it by clear-cutting. Of special concern is the cutting of old-growth forests. Studies have shown that old-growth forests provide crucial thermal cover to grizzlies and also supply potential den sites.

After an area is clear-cut, foresters often use herbicides to control the growth of unwanted vegetation. Unfortunately, the new vegetation is just what grizzlies thrive on — berries, devil's club, skunk cabbage, and other goodies. In 1991, a B.C. Environment, Lands and Parks study found that the use of herbicides can seriously affect the availability of grizzly foods over both the short and long terms. Over the short term, the grizzly's food supplies can be seriously reduced. Over

the long haul, dense stands of new trees can rob berry bushes and low growth of the sun they need to survive. Very few of the grizzly's favorite foods can make it under low-light conditions.

In response to queries on how to reduce the damage that logging in Canada has done to bear habitat, the World Wildlife Fund (Canada) has made the following suggestions:

- leaving half-mile strips on both sides of streams and rivers;
- avoiding intensive feeding areas like avalanche chutes and grassy meadows;
- leaving corridors of cover along roads and closing others altogether after logging to reduce the poaching that often follows the introduction of new roads in remote areas;
- using selective logging wherever possible as an alternative to clear-cutting or leaving islands of trees in cuts larger than twenty acres; and
- following strict procedures for garbage disposal by loggers.

Currently in British Columbia, *none* of these guidelines is being consistently followed. However, in June 1995, the B.C. Wildlife Branch finally announced a new conservation strategy for grizzlies, stating that "unless steps are taken now to conserve grizzly bear populations in British Columbia, this animal could disappear from our landscape forever."

A Grizzly Bear Scientific Committee set up under the strategy has made a long list of "hot spots" within British Columbia where the great bear is already in big trouble, including the Northern Cascades, Cabinet-Yaak, Pemberton, Granby-Kettle, Selkirks, Jumbo,

Babine, Elk Valley, and Cassiar areas. Grizzlies in the southern half of the province are described as suffering from particularly severe population declines.

In a seventy-page report, the branch recognized the effect that British Columbia's booming human population growth, the fastest in Canada, will have on grizzlies. The provincial population is expected to double by the year 2065, and as former B.C. Wildlife Branch director Ray Halliday admits, "more people means fewer bears."

The strategy recommends a system of protected areas, travel corridors, and no-hunting zones to preserve critical grizzly habitat. Suggested protected areas include the lower Stikine River, Kechika-Muskwa, southern Selkirk Mountains, and Kingcome Inlet areas. The strategy's ultimate objective "is to have one large core for each of the province's grizzly bear ecosystems and to ensure that these are linked with sufficient habitats to support grizzly bear populations."

The strategy also recommends additional research into provincial grizzly populations and habitats, rightly recognizing the need for hard facts on which to build management procedures. The research will be partly financed by a small surcharge to grizzly bear hunting licenses. Bear species licenses now include a Habitat Conservation Fund surcharge of $5 for B.C. hunters and $30 for non-resident hunters. The

surcharge is expected to raise about $160,000 a year for grizzly conservation efforts.

The government plans to improve public awareness about grizzlies through a new education program for schools and literature for target groups such as hunters and hikers. Two other recommendations are closer regulation of garbage disposal sites to reduce bear–human conflicts and increased enforcement and penalties for poachers.

Sunrise in the Mansell Valley.

As part of the grizzly conservation strategy, the B.C. Wildlife Branch is finally banning grizzly hunting in the Okanagan and southern Selkirk Mountains, where conservationists have called for such a ban for many years due to the small numbers of resident grizzlies. In 1993, conservationists were furious when fourteen grizzly hunting permits were allocated near Kokanee Glacier Park in the southern Selkirks. Bear biologists Wayne McCrory and Erica Mallum had found in a 1992 study that the area had almost three times the suggested 4 percent grizzly harvest figure and recommended an immediate closure of grizzly hunting to allow the population to recover. Their report was ignored.

Conservationists are pleased that the government is finally recognizing the fact that grizzlies are a high-risk species, but are critical that the plan may not be enough, a "too little, too late" situation. They also note that much of the conservation strategy consists merely of recommendations, which may or may not be followed. For example, although the strategy calls for increased enforcement, British Columbia is horribly understaffed when it comes to conservation officers, with only 136 field officers patrolling the entire province. Each officer covers an average territory of over three thousand square miles, an impossibly large area. According to the Raincoast Conservation Society, during all of 1995, conservation officers were in the field for only three days in the entire central British Columbia coastal area, where the coastal grizzly population has been halved due to trophy hunting, poaching, and habitat loss. Conservationists doubt that enough money can be found to effectively increase the conservation department; in recent years the number of field staff has actually been *decreasing*.

Conservationists also note that there are well over a hundred rural garbage dumps in central and northern British Columbia, plus hundreds of roadside garbage containers and recreation sites that do not have fencing of any sort or use bear-proof containers. Some of these dumps have chronic grizzly problems, such as those at New Aiyansh, Elkford, Revelstoke, Terrace, Stewart, and Kitimat. The dump at Mackenzie, in north-central British Columbia, used to be an especially severe problem; seventy bears near the dump were either killed or relocated within a one-year period prior to its closure. It is estimated that upgrading the northern rural dumps alone would cost well over half a million dollars. However, the conservation strategy has earmarked only $250,000 for improved waste control throughout the entire province.

Many people have also criticized the fact that proposed fines under the new plan are little more than a slap on the wrist to serious poachers. Under the new plan, the fines for a first poaching offense will be set at a minimum of $1,000 and a maximum of $25,000. Considering that judges usually assess a minimum fine for a first offense and that poachers can easily sell a grizzly gall bladder for up to $2,000 or a hide for up to $10,000, the new fines still seem low. In addition to stiffer fines, conservationists would like to see poachers receive jail sentences plus seizure of their arms, vehicles, boats, or aircraft used in poaching activities.

By October 1997, over two years after the new grizzly management plan was published, only partial progress on the grizzly management strategy had been accomplished by the provincial government.

A Scientific Committee has been formed to advise the B.C. Wildlife Branch on technical aspects of grizzly management; it consists of over a dozen well-respected grizzly biologists from Canada and the United States. (Attempts by the Guide Outfitters Association of

British Columbia to place one of its pro-hunting members on the Committee have proved unsuccessful; one of its representatives tried to attend the April 26, 1996, meeting of the Committee and "voluntarily left the meeting" after being requested to do so.)

A Conflict Management Committee has been established to advise on the development of improved waste disposal sites, and seventeen sites have had electric fences installed, including those at Kitimat, Stewart, Revelstoke, Elkford, New Aiyansh, and Terrace. (Although secure garbage disposal sites are a good start, there continues to be much criticism of the government's handling of bear–human conflicts; the Scientific Committee has noted that "there is a strong movement within COs [conservation officers] to shoot all bears near communities."

(Above) Bunchberry, or dwarf dogwood, a beautiful fall flower found in the Mansell Valley. (Opposite) Shades of lemon and lime dapple the forest floor in September.

A Grizzly Bear Trust Fund has been set up, containing over $140,000 through the sale of calendars and through public donations. But no new protected areas or travel corridors for grizzlies have been established, no additional conservation officers have been hired, and a promised Forest Practices Code field guide for grizzlies has yet to be written. (The guide is going to be incorporated into the Managing Identified Wildlife Guidebook, which has not yet been approved.)

Perhaps most importantly, much more effort still has to be made to protect populations of grizzlies identified as threatened. For example, only twenty to thirty grizzlies are left in the Granby Park area of southern British Columbia. In 1990, they were the first grizzly population in Canada to be nationally identified as threatened. And so conservationists were shocked when eighteen logging cutblocks were approved in 1996 in the Goatskin Special Resource Management Zone near Granby Park. In the mad rush for dollars, the grizzlies were once again forgotten.

Few conservationists believe that the forestry business will suddenly change its ways to help the grizzly. Unfortunately, the new conservation strategy states that the designation of Grizzly Bear Management Areas "will not necessarily prohibit resource extraction."

And even more unfortunate is the fact that existing forestry regulations are frequently ignored in remote areas of British Columbia where inspections are few and far between. In my first three years of living in a remote area of central British Columbia, I saw numerous incidences of improper garbage disposal by loggers, "controlled" burns that soon got out of control due to inadequate supervision, illegal clear-cuts taken right to the edge of critical salmon streams, improperly prepared logging roads, and flagrant violations of replanting regulations. All of these infractions could have negative impacts on grizzly populations. Although a number of logging companies are finally being charged for their forestry offenses, forestry is a multi-billion-dollar industry in British Columbia, and the attraction of big bucks will always outweigh the inherent rights of wild animals.

Across the rest of North America, forestry practices and other factors have destroyed much of the grizzly bear's habitat. But an audacious plan known as the Yellowstone to Yukon Conservation Initiative (Y2Y) seeks to remedy that, envisaging an 1,800-mile spread of connected parks stretching from Yellowstone National Park to the Yukon.

The initiative had its origins in a classic 1967 book by biologists Robert MacArthur and Edward O. Wilson entitled *The Theory of Island Biogeography.* In the book, MacArthur and Wilson discussed their discovery that island plant and animal communities are more subject to extinction than non-island species, a simple concept that proved to have far-reaching implications.

In the 1970s, biologist Michael Soulé extrapolated the MacArthur–Wilson concept to land-based ecosystems. He asserted that clear-cuts, private ranches, highways, and urban sprawl are just as limiting to terrestrial species as the ocean is to island-based species. And he wondered if the isolated groups of animals living in established parks and preserves across North America were facing the same high extinction rate as island species. His ideas were hotly debated at the First International Conference on Conservation Biology, held in San Diego in 1978, and a ripple of concern spread across the continent.

In 1990, the World Wildlife Fund (Canada) released its Conservation Strategy for Large Carnivores in Canada. Since carnivores are at the top of the food chain, the general health of carnivore populations can be an indicator of the health of the rest of the entire ecosystem. The strategy recommended the establishment of Carnivore Conservation Areas, adding pointedly "we must also keep in mind the importance of linking them."

In 1993 discussions between Soulé and Dave Foreman, cofounder of the radical conservation group, Earth First!, led to the establishment of The Wildlands Project, a group dedicated to the idea of linking up the parks and preserves along the rocky spine of the continent, where the highest concentrations of large carnivores remain. The project's mission statement states poignantly: "We live for the day when Grizzlies in Chihuahua [Mexico] have an unbroken connection to Grizzlies in Alaska." One of the main goals of The Wildlands Project is the Y2Y initiative.

In October 1997, over three hundred biologists gathered in Waterton National Park and ratified the Y2Y initiative as a dream worth pursuing. As a campaign symbol for the initiative, the biologists chose the grizzly.

Part science, part dream, the Y2Y project is years from fruition. It is a bold idea, but the logistics are daunting. To establish wildlife corridors between parks would require the cooperation of a long list of local, regional, provincial, state, territorial, and federal agencies on both sides of the Canada–United States border. And some of the gaps between existing parks are huge. Between the Yellowstone ecosystem in Montana and the Selway-Bitterroot system in Idaho is a gap of 240 miles. Over 200 miles exist between the new Muskwa-Kechika provincial park in northern British Columbia and the Willmore-Jasper-Banff park complex in Alberta. The Castle Wilderness gap north of Waterton National Park and south of Peter Lougheed Provincial Park in Alberta is almost as long. It is of special

The preservation of the grizzly's future depends on preservation of habitat.

concern, for in recent years the Castle Wilderness has been the site of many grizzly and wolf shootings.

Some biologists fear that the complex of political jurisdictions involved in the initiative will kill the dream before it begins. They point to the years of delay in the reintroduction of wolves to Yellowstone caused by squabbling between Montana state biologists and the federal U.S. Fish and Wildlife Service. Others point

to that same project with pride and to the lessons of cooperation among biologists that it provided. As biologist Dian Fossey wrote in *Gorillas in the Mist,* "When you realize the value of all life, you dwell less on what is past and concentrate more on the preservation of the future."

For the grizzly to even have a future, a secure habitat is not merely a dream. It is an absolute necessity.

Seven

WAITING FOR WINTER

BY EARLY OCTOBER, THE SALMON RUNS WERE OVER, AND THE riverbanks were littered with the spent bodies of spawned-out salmon. The pronounced hook on the males' noses gave the carcasses a distinct dog-like appearance, and with the gums peeled back by the hand of death to reveal a mouthful of sharp teeth, the dead fish looked very fierce indeed.

But from death comes life, and the hundreds of salmon carcasses will feed hundreds of other plant and animal species, as well as enriching the waters for future generations of salmon. Thickets of willows, hatchet-headed mergansers, clouds of hovering dragonflies — all are fed by the nitrogen, the protein, and the minerals that ooze from the dead salmon. In some parts of Washington, biologists even add more salmon carcasses to the banks of salmon streams as fodder for the juvenile salmon that will hatch the following spring, completing yet another of nature's miraculous circles.

To the Terror Twins, the dead fish made handy toys. I once saw one of the twins grab a dead salmon and then hop onto a beached tree trunk where he danced above his brother, teasing him with the carcass. When the cub on the ground looked the other way, the cub on the trunk suddenly jumped down on top of him, a sibling slam-dunk, bear-style. The two then ran off playfully down the Salmon Bar, only to be brought back by a sharp woof from their mother. She wasn't pleased with their antics and gave one cub a swat with her mighty paw. The poor

(Above) The dappled golds of a Mansell autumn. (Opposite) Hoarfrost drapes the trees by late September.

(Opposite) The Terror Twins.
(Right) A gory battle between
snake and frog.

cub squealed once and then edged up to her, uttering a strange gurgling sound and twisting his rear end toward her in an obvious submissive or repentant gesture. I've seen one of my own dogs use the same movement after she adds yet another spot to my living-room carpet.

Watching all of this was another bear, a big female whom I called Chuckles. Chuckles had a permanent half-smile on her face like some hairy Mona Lisa, and her roly-poly figure seemed to fit her jovial facial expression. This big dumpling of a bear watched the Twins play with the dead fish with great interest, probably hoping they would drop it. Or maybe she

really did find them amusing — with that fixed smile on her fat face, I just couldn't tell.

Academics will scoff at such notions, declaring loftily that animals do not show the same emotions that humans do. I couldn't agree less; I can tell instantly if my dogs are happy or sad, for example, just by looking at their faces. And when my horse nods his head and prances off, kicking up his heels, I know that he is feeling pleased with life. I don't know why scientists are loath to admit animal emotions; perhaps it is because the lines between humans and animals have become so blurred as more and more research accumulates.

(Opposite) Chuckles.

(Left) A hooded merganser.

It used to be that the distinction was intelligence, and intelligence was measured by tool-use. In my grandmother's day, it was stated that humans are the only animals that could make and use tools. But we now know that many wild animals make and use tools. For example, chimpanzees strip twigs to use as fishing poles in anthills, and some species of birds choose angular rocks to help them break open other birds' eggs or sharp thorns to pry grubs out of trees.

Then many scientists stated dogmatically that the cognitive use of language is the sole domain of humans. But in 1967, a chimp named Washoe, trained in American Sign Language, signed to her trainers, "Gimme sweet." Since then a long list of other chimpanzees and a couple of gorillas have shown an amazing grasp of sentence structure and construction.

So perhaps emotion is one of the few guidelines left to scientists to prove our "superiority" over the beasts. How arrogant our need for such assurance is in the first place. I hope the day will soon come when we learn to share the Earth, to drop our colonial attitude toward other species and accept them as siblings deserving of our respect.

On the lake where I lived for three years I once found a juvenile bald eagle that had its legs twisted up in fishing line. Many times I have found discarded line

along the beaches of that lake, left by some thoughtless angler. I have even found fishing lines attached to poles and planted along the shore on purpose, to be retrieved at some later date. The unfortunate eaglet had likely come from a big nest at the north end of the lake and had probably plunged his talons into a dead fish on the end of one of these planted lines. The bird was flapping around in the shallows and was obviously very weak.

I knew from my experience volunteering at a raptor rehabilitation center that the mighty talons were the part of the bird to be reckoned with, so I took off my shirt and held it out for the bird to grab. When it lashed out and grabbed the shirt with one foot, I quickly wrapped the rest of the shirt around both feet and cut the fishing line wrapped around the bird's legs with a small pocket knife.

The line had cut deep into the bird's flesh, but no bones were broken. Often the stress of capture is more damaging than an injury itself, so I just washed off the cuts with lake water and let the bird go. It sat stock-still for a few minutes and then laboriously flew away, hopefully a bit wiser in the process.

Had I done the right thing? Many people would criticize me for interfering with nature and in the same position would have let the bird die. But I'll always remember the words of biologist Jane Goodall when she was asked why she interfered and gave medicine to her beloved chimpanzees when they were stricken with polio. "If they had been humans," she said, "no one would have ever questioned my actions. What difference does it make that they were animals?"

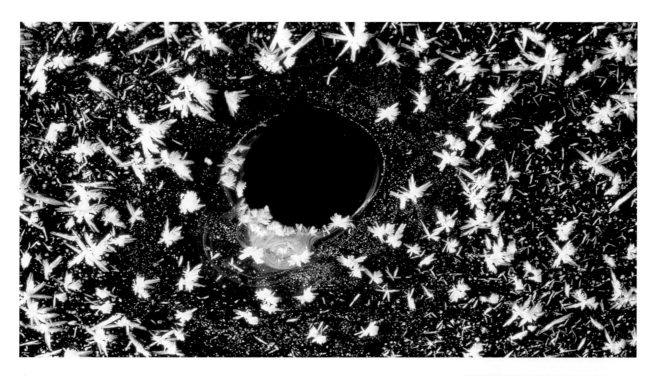

(Above) One of the last holes in the ice
on the Mansell River, surrounded by an
abstract splatter of frost shards. (Right)
October 15 — the first snow in the
Mansell Valley. (Opposite) Hoarfrost
turns trees into crystalline sculptures.

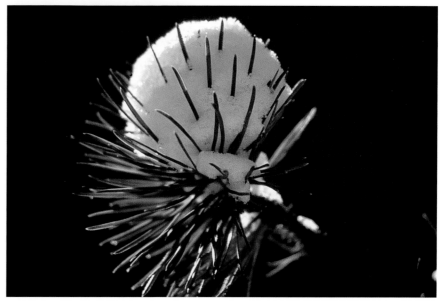

By mid-October, my bear-sighting days wound down as the grizzlies headed for the hills to search out cozy dens for winter. The Terror Twins and their mother were the first to go, followed by the subadults. The adult bears were the last to leave. The last gasp of summer was stifled by increasingly cold nights, and some mornings when I arrived at the bar the land was blanketed with a fairy-land covering of hoarfrost. When I walked through the bushes, the crystalline shards of frost would tinkle like glass wind chimes, a strangely feminine sound in so masculine a landscape. On the last hike out, my head was full of questions. Where exactly did all the bears go? How far away were their dens? Would all the cubs survive the winter? And how many would be back next year?

The first snowfall was a shock, for it came down not in a light sprinkle, but in a wholesale whitewashing of the land. And that sparkling coating brought an unexpected bonus in the number of animal tracks it revealed. The snow, for example, clearly showed the squirrel highways that ran between trees, verifying that the busy beasts used the same direct paths over and over again.

I was pleased to see wolf tracks one morning on my trail into the valley. Pleased not only that I saw the tracks, but also that the beleaguered wolves had taken refuge in the valley alongside the great bears.

The stark white background also allowed me a glimpse of one of the rarest of predators. It looked like a huge weasel loping along with the curious humpbacked, looping gait that weasels use. But it was the size of a cocker spaniel, and the only member of the weasel family that large is the wolverine.

Perhaps no other forest denizen has such a reputation for viciousness as the wolverine. Occasionally a wolverine will drive a grizzly off its kill, but more often the big bear comes out on top in these face-offs. As with many other species, much of what we "know" about the wolverine is a muddled mix of campfire stories and outright tall tales.

I can attest, though, to the strength of the wolverine. I worked one summer many years ago in the Yukon, where I did field geology from fly camps deep in the Yukon woods. Often on my traverses I would come across prospectors' cabins, and I once found a cabin that had been raided by a wolverine. The brass door knob on the cabin had been wrenched right off the door by the wolverine's mighty jaws, and the inside of the cabin looked like a tornado had hit it.

In February 1997, I helped three biologists working on a wolverine and fisher study in the remote Omineca Mountains of northern British Columbia. The heaviest wolverine that we live-trapped was an old thirty-six-pound male that we named Big Bob. Bob's teeth showed the rigors of life in the wild: he had four broken canines, all of his upper incisors were chipped, and his lower incisors were very worn. And yet, after recovering from his tranquilizer for radio-collaring, Big Bob gnawed through a frozen moose leg

(Above) Winter extends its icy grip early in the Mansell Valley. (Opposite) Despite the appearance of this young male, the wolverine's reputation for viciousness is greatly exaggerated.

and reduced the big femur bone inside to a pile of splinters. Their jaw strength, even with a mouthful of broken teeth, is simply awesome.

As far as viciousness goes, I found the wolverine no more vicious than most predators, preferring to flee from humans whenever possible. In a live trap, the wolverine emits a deep throaty growl that sounds quite impressive, but the most vicious sound comes from live-trapped martens, which give out a high-pitched scream. From the volume of the sound, I often expected to see a big wild cat when I opened the trap door, not a half-pound marten.

Grumpy was one of the last bears to leave the Salmon Bar. As the other adults slowly trickled away into the mountains, he took advantage of their absence, frantically scrounging a few last fish from fishing sites he wouldn't have dared to use before. Sometimes he stood on a large rock, facing upstream and holding his nose up into the wind, inhaling great lungfuls of the cold, crisp air. Was he sniffing for bear scent, still fearing the return of the more dominant bears? Or was he seeking some chemical message in the air to trigger his own departure? For whatever reason, there finally came the day when he, too, was gone. Alone on the Salmon Bar, I felt like a kid whose friends had deserted him on the playground.

At the end of October, on one of my last trips into the valley, I stumbled along, thinking more than looking, when I suddenly stopped and stared at the ground. There, amidst the leafy litter, lay a cigarette butt. I don't smoke. I stared down at the butt for a couple of long, agonizing minutes.

Man had arrived in the Mansell River Valley.

Gazing toward an uncertain future.

Epilogue

All life has bounds, constraints that put some type of restrictions on our lives. But for wild animals, man-made constraints now rule their wild worlds. Grizzlies, like most other animals, are being pushed into smaller and smaller habitats. Soon they may have nowhere at all to go.

In late 1996, two major logging companies announced plans to clear-cut additional blocks in central British Columbia. One of the blocks lies just half a mile from the Valley of the Grizzlies.

Appendix
How to Act in Grizzly Country

Many early books on grizzlies declared that it was the unpredictable nature of the grizzly that made it a force to be reckoned with in the woods. Today, however, that attitude is changing. Jim Faro, a biologist with the Alaska Department of Fish and Game, says: "The term 'unpredictable' only means our knowledge is incomplete." The average person's knowledge about grizzlies used to be based on hunting lore and fireside stories; today, those fables and exaggerations are being replaced by fact, and more knowledge is emerging about how to act in grizzly country.

One of the most dangerous bear situations is the surprise close-range encounter, especially if the bear has cubs or is at a kill site. It is important to be alert in bear country: watch for bear tracks, scat, day beds, diggings, overturned boulders, and scratched or rubbed trees. Any fresh signs should send up a red flag that it might be wise to back off. It is definitely unwise to check out the smell of rotting meat: grizzlies defend their kills quickly and viciously. The sight of crows, ravens, and other birds congregating in one spot, which may be the result of a kill site on the ground below, is also a sign to avoid the area.

Be careful to avoid high-risk areas such as game trails in thick brush or beside salmon streams. Other areas to avoid are avalanche chutes in spring and early summer and burned-over areas, all of which are favorite grizzly feeding areas.

In many cases, the decision the bear makes on attacking or not attacking depends on distance: the closer you are, the worse your chances. One of the best defenses, therefore, if a grizzly is suddenly spotted is to slowly back off. In closer encounters, many authorities recommend standing still, but looking off to one side to avoid eye contact. Never run, for almost any animal will chase a moving target.

Sometimes, a grizzly will charge. Luckily, most charges are bluffs, moves intended to drive the intruder out of a bear's territory. Sadly, many hunters panic when charged, and many grizzlies are needlessly shot as a result. In fact, in his recent book on bear attacks, *Bear Encounter Survival Guide,* bear hunter James Gary Shelton even recommends always shooting grizzlies when they are closer than eighty-two feet (it's not clear how he came up with this number) and when "a carcass is nearby . . . or where cubs accidentally run towards you" or "if a bear comes at you in a low, crouched run" or in "a surprise close-range encounter with any bear." I have had many encounters with grizzlies closer than eighty-two feet, and have never had to shoot any of them. Unfortunately, the author of these heavy-handed guidelines is now giving bear-defense courses to government personnel in British Columbia.

According to the latest research by grizzly biologist Stephen Herrero, in the case of an actual attack the best defense is lying face down, fingers interlaced behind the neck. As he writes, "serious injury in such incidents is often focused on the face." The benefits of such advice were recognized as early as 1806, when explorer Simon Fraser wrote of a native woman attacked by a grizzly: "she instantly laid down flat upon the ground and did not stir, in consequence of [which] the bear deserted [her]." More recent corroboration comes from a tragic attack in 1976 in Glacier National Park. When a grizzly attacked one hiker, he resisted for a while and then played dead, placing his hands behind his head. Only then did the bear drop him and attack a second hiker, who resisted and was killed.

The exception to the rule of lying still comes when hikers are attacked while sleeping outdoors. These attacks are not the result of a bear being surprised on the trail, defending cubs, or defending prey. Rather, they are the result of predation, often cases of a bear looking for something to eat in a campground full of food smells. Some biologists believe that the horizontal attitude of sleeping campers reminds the bear of wounded or dead prey lying on the ground. In these cases, Herrero recommends: "Shout at the bear. Throw things at or near it so you can escape. Use every possible weapon or repellent you might have." Often the bear will get the message and will leave you with little more than a ripped tent, torn sleeping bag, and one heck of a story to tell upon your arrival back home.

Opinions are mixed about the hot-pepper sprays currently available on the market as bear repellents. As one biologist put it, "if a charging grizzly is so close that you can spray it in the face, the game is over to begin with." Others are worried that the sprays might give some hikers a sense of false security, causing them to forget common sense in bear country. National park warden Hal Morrison warns that "it's just a tool to help," and is concerned that some hikers may get the attitude that "'I can whip any bear that I see.'" Morrison himself has used the spray on a charging grizzly he encountered in Larch Valley near Banff, Alberta, a popular hiking area. "Most of it missed him but . . . the loud aerosol hiss deterred him," he says.

American hikers in Canada should note that it is illegal to bring sprays with mace as the main ingredient, or sprays also intended for use on humans, into the country. The active ingredient in most bear sprays, however, is not mace but capsicum, which is derived from red peppers. This substance irritates both the eyes and nasal passages of a bear, incapacitating it for about five minutes if it receives a direct blast. Bears get rid of the substance by rolling in wet grass or in water, and it causes no permanent damage.

Bear sprays were first developed in 1980 by Bill Pounds, an American inventor. They reached the market in 1986, under such names as Standoff, Counter Assault, Assault Guard, Bear Guard, Bear Scare, and many others. John Eisenhauer, a biologist involved in the development of Standoff, hopes that the spray may help condition problem bears to avoid humans. In some cases, though, the opposite seems to be happening. Jim Hart, a conservation officer in Fort Nelson, British Columbia, has reported that some of the nuisance black bears in his area have been sprayed many times and have become partially resistant to the spray.

Many people are concerned about the potential misuse of bear sprays. Wildlife photographer Michael Francis voices these feelings: "People must be very careful with this spray and not push their luck in getting too close to bears just because they have the spray with them." Of course, use bear sprays only at close quarters and remember that they can be blown away by wind. (Many of the cans carry suggestions that you make sure the bear is downwind before spraying it, but few people have the time or presence of mind for such maneuvering in an attack situation.) It is not recommended to test the can after purchasing it; there are many reports of cans slowly losing their pressure after such tests. And the spray cans have a limited volume, usually containing only enough spray for five or six two-second bursts. Many people now suggest carrying two cans so that one can be used in each hand.

Opinions are also mixed on the use of flares against a charging grizzly. They don't always work, for one thing. In many cases, their use has resulted in accidental grass fires; as a result, flares have been banned in many parks.

The supposed advantages of bear bells are a little more encouraging. In one study in Glacier National Park, only one hiker in four was found to be wearing bear bells, but of all the hikers charged by grizzlies, not one was carrying a bell. However, in dense brush, or near rushing water, the delicate sounds of bells may not be loud enough. Stephen Herrero loudly yodels in bear country, adding a "short, explosive high-pitched sound at the end." Other people have even carried airhorns into bear country, especially when they have expected thick brush conditions.

Personally, I hate the irritating sound of tinkling bells in the wilderness. It always sounds like the Good Humor man has somehow followed me into the woods. So while in grizzly country, I sing instead. My favorite tune is the theme from *The Bridge on the River Kwai*, using da-da-da as the words. (And my singing will scare off anything.)

Don't use a single high-pitched whistle in alpine areas, as this sound is very similar to the call of the marmot and often *attracts* grizzlies. (Unfortunately, many Canadian parks brochures still recommend using a sharp whistle, although the potential problems have been pointed out to them many times.) Some outdoorsmen now suggest that all yodels or yells in bear country be repeated at least once, as many animals wait for a second sound before fleeing.

Never go alone into grizzly country; larger groups of people make more noise, and in the case of an attack, companions may be able to drive off a bear or summon help. Also, it's best to avoid hiking at dusk or dawn, as these are times when bears actively feed.

Most authorities recommend that dogs never be taken into grizzly country on the basis that a dog being chased by a bear might bring it right back to the dog's owner. However, I know of two cases in which dogs have driven off attacking grizzlies and I have heard of other cases in which just the sound of a barking dog was enough to scare off an inquisitive bear. Perhaps the best advice is to keep a dog on a leash. Aside from keeping the dog out of bear trouble, a leash will also keep a dog from chasing or killing other wildlife.

If an aggressive bear or a bear that shows absolutely no fear of humans is encountered, report it as soon as possible to the nearest park warden or ranger. Most park officials take such reports very seriously, and will close hiking trails or campsites to prevent potential problems.

Simple camping precautions can stop most grizzly attacks. For example, strong-smelling meat such as bacon or fish is a poor choice for campers in grizzly country. Powdered or dried foods are less likely to attract predators and are lighter to carry. Keep all food and garbage in tight air-proof containers or suspended above a bear's reach, or better yet, both. If your vehicle is nearby, lock the food in the trunk. It's also a good idea to sleep as far away from the cooking area as possible.

Garbage should be burned or packed out; burying it isn't good enough in bear country. Grizzlies have a tremendous sense of smell (about seventy-five times that of most humans), and the last thing this country needs is more bears used to eating human garbage.

Hunters must also take special care in grizzly country. Fresh meat should be suspended at least ten feet off the ground. One Wyoming outfitter thoughtlessly left his meat in saddlebags packed onto his horse, which was tied to a tree. Both the meat and the horse were taken by a hungry grizzly. Sleeping tents should be located well away from the meat. Gut piles should be burned, placed in airtight containers, and packed out. And hunters shouldn't hang around after a kill; fresh meat should be hauled out of grizzly country quickly as the smell will attract bears from miles around. Hunters should be alert when hiking out with the meat; to a hungry grizzly, a hunter with a backpack full of meat is just an appetizing entrée on two legs.

Following these simple, commonsense rules in bear country reduces the chances of an encounter with an aggressive grizzly. And remember, a clean camp is a bear-free camp.

Selected Bibliography

Brown, Gary. *The Great Bear Almanac.* New York: Lyons & Burford, 1993.

Dufresne, Frank. *No Room for Bears.* Anchorage: Alaska Northwest Books, 1991.

Herrero, Stephen. *Bear Attacks: Their Causes and Avoidance.* New York: Lyons & Burford, 1988.

Hummel, Monte, and Sherry Pettigrew. *Wild Hunters: Predators in Peril.* Toronto: World Wildlife Fund (Canada) and Key Porter Books Limited, 1991.

Leopold, Aldo. *A Sand County Almanac.* New York: Oxford University Press, Inc., 1949.

McNamee, Thomas. *The Grizzly Bear.* New York: Alfred A. Knopf, Inc., 1984.

Murie, Adolph. *A Naturalist in Alaska.* New York: Devin Adair, 1961.

Nelson, Richard K. *Make Prayers to the Raven.* Chicago: University of Chicago Press, 1983.

Peacock, Doug. *Grizzly Years.* New York: Henry Holt and Company, Inc., 1990.

Quammen, David. *The Song of the Dodo.* New York: Simon and Schuster Inc., 1996.

Russell, Andy. *Grizzly Country.* New York: Alfred A. Knopf, Inc., 1967.

Walker, Tom. *River of Bears.* Stillwater, Minnesota: Voyageur Press Inc., 1993.

Whitaker, John O., Jr. *The Audubon Society Field Guide to North American Mammals.* New York: Alfred A. Knopf, Inc., 1980.